KU-740-339

Essential
Normandy

by

ROBERT KANE

Robert Kane is an art historian specialising in
Renaissance poetry, art and architecture. He has
written several guides to Italy and holidays regularly in
Normandy

AA

Produced by AA Publishing

Written by Robert Kane
Verified by Robert Kane
Peace and Quiet section by
Paul Sterry

Revised second edition 1996
First published 1993

Edited, designed and produced
by AA Publishing.
© The Automobile Association
1993, 1996
Maps © The Automobile
Association 1993, 1996 .

Distributed in the United Kingdom
by AA Publishing, Norfolk House,
Priestley Road, Basingstoke,
Hampshire, RG24 9NY.

A CIP catalogue record for this
book is available from the British
Library.

ISBN 0 7495 1319 5

Published by AA Publishing, a
trading name of Automobile
Association Developments
Limited, whose registered office is
Norfolk House, Priestley Road,
Basingstoke, Hampshire,
RG24 9NY.
Registered number 1878835.

Colour separation: BTB Colour
Reproduction Ltd., Whitchurch,
Hampshire.

Printed by: Printers S.R.L., Trento,
Italy

Front cover picture: *Mont-St-
Michel*

Contents

This book employs a simple rating system to help choose which places to visit:

✓	'top ten' sights

◆◆◆	do not miss
◆◆	see if you can
◆	worth seeing if you have time

Introduction and Background

INTRODUCTION

Normandy is one of the largest regions of France and full of variety. Towards its eastern end it borders on the suburbs of Paris, and its capital, Rouen, straddles Paris's river, the Seine. Much of the Normandy coast is Paris's playground: the rich go to Deauville, with its race-course and its long, straight beach of perfect yellow sand, while other Parisians go year after year to their houses, favourite family hotels, chalets or caravans scattered along the

The Porte des Cordeliers in the town walls at Falaise, birthplace of William the Conqueror

almost endless coast. Here, in summer, they will mingle with visitors of every nationality, the British above all but also many Germans, Dutch, Belgians and Italians.

This is the Normandy of the old-fashioned family holiday, with all the joy of a northern temperate zone summer. Normandy caters for it brilliantly. The coast has the beaches, cliffs and harbours, the isolated, forgotten spots, the old-fashioned resorts. Even if it has no mountains, Normandy has vales and rivers, orchards and pastures, hundreds of old farmsteads, many abbeys, and more castles, *châteaux*, churches, museums and gardens than you can possibly visit.

Many of these places recall Normandy's history. For the French, this was once a wild region, outside the pale of the Ile-de-France, a land occupied by the Norsemen and not finally conquered until the second half of the 15th century. For the British it is a land of origins – birthplace of William the Conqueror, site of the Bayeux tapestry, source of the Caen stone with which many English churches were built,

and the perfect setting for towering medieval walls of the kind associated with Shakespeare's Henry V.

For other people Normandy will be associated particularly with the Impressionist painters, who came on their own family holidays to a coast made newly accessible by the railway. Many of the resorts and landmarks they painted have changed little. Despite the oil refinery at Le Havre and the industry straddling the Seine up to Rouen, despite the destruction wrought during the 1944 Allied invasion, Normandy is an unspoilt land. It has not budged from its traditions, and is more homely and hospitable than many other parts of France.

Normandy (Normandie) can be divided into east and west, conventionally known as Upper (Haute) and Lower (Basse). In fact, apart from the sea, it has only one strong natural boundary – the River Seine, which cleaves Upper Normandy in two and has been bridged below Rouen only in the last 20 years. Northern Upper Normandy, the administrative *département* of Seine Maritime, includes the coastal ports and resorts of Dieppe, Fécamp, Etretat and Le Havre, and has its capital at Rouen, with its historic centre on the north bank of the Seine. Known as the Pays de Caux, this is a region to itself, while the rest of Normandy – comprising the four *départements* of Eure, Orne, Calvados and Manche – extends over forest and farmland, between a dense pattern of small towns (and a few large ones), without any obvious break. Only a shallow chain of hills separates it from the Loire Valley region to the south. However, the countryside tends to become rather less lush as you go further westwards, into the *département* of Manche. The Cotentin (Cherbourg) Peninsula is wild and rugged at its northern tip, but the southern extremity of Manche is low-lying and marshy, except for the isolated rock of Mont-St-Michel. Historically, Normandy has only two capital towns, Caen (in Calvados) in Lower Normandy and Rouen (in Seine Maritime) in Upper Normandy. Heavy industry is essentially limited to the valley of the Seine, though Caen is a steel town and a number of nuclear power-

Boats at Cherbourg

stations have been built along the coasts. One motorway, the A13, comes down the Seine from Paris, passes to the south of Rouen, and dies out at Caen, though dual carriageway extends to Bayeux and in patches up to the important port of Cherbourg. Travellers from the Channel Tunnel and the Channel ports can now connect with the A13 on a new dual carriageway between Dieppe and Rouen, also branching across to Le Havre. The rest of Normandy is not on the way to anywhere, but abounds in country roads and local traffic, shuttling between the various villages and small towns about its own business.

Normandy is almost always reached by land or sea (through the ports of Cherbourg, Caen, Le Havre and Dieppe). This has helped the region to keep its character and its own tastes, for instance in its architecture or in its food. It still serves, for instance, the kind of cream-sauce dishes that the new cuisine has driven out elsewhere, not to mention its fish and shellfish still caught, sold and eaten the same day. It has a largely land-bound or peasant population unswayed by changing fashions or the big city, though opportunistic enough to prosper.

Bathing at Trouville, 1884. Family holidays are a long-established tradition on the Normandy coast

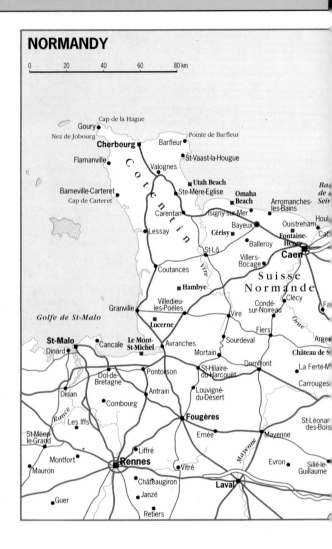

NORMANDY

0   20   40   60   80 km

Cap de la Hague
Goury
Nez de Jobourg   Pointe de Barfleur
Cherbourg   Barfleur
Flamanville   St-Vaast-la-Hougue
                    Valognes
                                ■ **Utah Beach**
Barneville-Carteret   Ste-Mère-Eglise   **Omaha**   *Ba*
Cap de Carteret   ■ **Beach**   *de*
                                        Arromanches-   *Sein*
                        Carentan   Isigny-sur-Mer   les-Bains
                                        Houl
                                Bayeux   Ouistreham
            Lessay   **Cérisy** ■   Cab
                        ■ Balleroy   **Fontaine-**
                        St-Lô   **Henry**
                                        Caen
                                Villers-
            Coutances   Bocage   *Suisse*
                                            Normande
                    ■ **Hambye**   Clécy
                    Villedieu-   Condé-   *Fa*
    Golfe de St-Malo Granville les-Poêles Vire sur-Noireau   *Orne*
                        Lucerne   Flers
                                            Arge
    St-Malo   Le Mont-   Avranches Sourdeval   **Château de S**
    Dinard ● Cancale **St-Michel**   La Ferté-M
                        Pontorson Mortain   Domfront
        Dinan   Dol-de-   St-Hilaire-   Carrouges
                    Bretagne   du-Harcouët
                        Antrain   Louvigné-
            Combourg   du-Désert   St-Léonar
    Rance   des-Bois
    St-Méen- Les Iffs   **Fougères**
    le-Grand   Ernée   Mayenne
        Montfort   ● Liffré   Evron ●   Sillé-le-
    Mauron   **Rennes** ● Vitré   *Mayenne*   Guillaume
                    Châteaugiron
        Guer   Janzé   **Laval**
                    Retiers

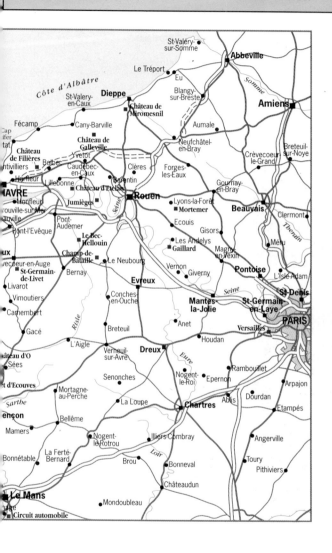

BACKGROUND

Early history

Before it was Norman, Normandy was part of
the vast Celtic commonwealth of 'tribes' (as the
Romans called them) with close relations not
only to the rest of Gaul but also across the
water to England. During the Bronze Age tin
from Cornwall was imported up the River
Seine, but otherwise few traces remain of
settlement in 'Armorica' (Upper Normandy and
Brittany) before the Roman conquest. Nor is
there any trace of the little Gaulish village in
which the comic-strip character Astérix once
lived, though it is meant to be somewhere on
this coast!

Once Gaul had been conquered by Julius
Caesar in the mid-1st century BC, towns were
founded at nodal sites, some of which survived
the Dark Ages and remain Normandy's capitals
today. Rotomagus became Rouen,
Caracotinum became Harfleur (now engulfed
in Le Havre), Mediolanum became Evreux,
Cosedia/Constantia became Coutances.
Others had little posterity, for instance
Juliobona (modern Lillebonne) or Noviodunum
(Jublains, near Mayenne, just to the south of
modern Normandy), and at these, accordingly,
there is still something Roman to see. The
archaeological sections of the museums at
Rouen and Evreux display fragments, artefacts
and models.

Normandy's Dark Ages were very dark.
Scarcely a name or a legend has survived from
that time between the 4th and the 9th centuries
when invaders and raiders, first Saxons then
Norsemen, had their will of the country, both
along the coast and inland as they made their
way up the many navigable rivers. Most of
Normandy, of course, remained impenetrable
forest. Frankish rule under Clovis at the
beginning of the 6th century extended down
the Seine, but reached no further westwards –
however, there had been a glimmer of life at
Sées (north of Alençon) under Bishop St Latuin
in the early 5th century, and in the early 8th
century, in the extreme west, St Aubert was
induced to get up from Avranches and found
Mont-St-Michel.

Bayeux Cathedral

The Norman Achievement

The establishment of medieval Normandy was
the work of Rollo, Normandy's first duke or *dux*
– the Byzantine term for an autonomous
military governor. In 911 he agreed with
Charles the Simple of France to cease raiding
beyond the Seine tributaries Epte (to the north)
and Avre (to the south), which have remained
the borders of Normandy ever since. Rollo,
too, was the first of the Norsemen or Vikings to
settle, making Rouen his capital. The early
development of the dukedom of the Norsemen
or *Normands* as the French called them was
centred, not surprisingly, around the timeless
highway of the Seine.

The 10th century, if only more were known
about it, was a vital period of transformation in
Normandy. More swiftly and effectively than
the old Carolingian centres, the dukedom
developed as an organised state and as a focus
of that main vehicle of civilisation for the high
Middle Ages, monasticism. While outstanding
intellects of the day, such as Lanfranc from
northern Italy, came here to join the flourishing
abbeys, the Normans themselves set off in
numbers to conquer the world. The Normans
of this period demonstrated a genius for the
two great requirements of the age, worship
and warfare. The latter involved not just
berserk Viking bravery, but strategic and
technological innovations, while the former
was not merely about singing and copying
ancient manuscripts, but included composing
and building. Above all the Normans were
builders, of the new-fangled motte-and-bailey
castles and of churches in a new style and
technique called Romanesque.

As in the case of Bayeux Cathedral, mostly
rebuilt in the 13th century, few Norman
churches of the early, formative period have
survived, but, as well as Lessay in the Cotentin,
two great exceptions are the Abbaye aux
Hommes, founded at Caen by William in the
year of the Conquest, and the still earlier
abbey at Jumièges on the Seine. Jumièges is
itself said to be dependent on the Norman-style
cathedral built at Westminster in London about
1050 by Edward the Confessor, now lost. But at
Jumièges there are both signs of throwbacks to

Carolingian architecture, the Normans' starting point, and some novelties, developed more strongly at Caen.

Essentially, the Normans inherited churches conceived loosely as long halls with pierced walls, and developed instead the idea of a rigid, almost mathematical structure composed of identical repeating units. Hence early Norman Romanesque, even though massive and primitive, also has a marvellous regularity and purity.

It was the cultural and technical as much as the military prowess of the Normans that enabled Duke William (1028–1087) to conquer and to hold England. He arrived not as an adventurist but as a legitimate claimant whom the previous king, Edward the Confessor, had honoured and to whom, according to the Bayeux tapestry, he had wished to leave the throne. The Bayeux tapestry, reflecting largely Anglo-Saxon skills in depiction and narration, is itself a sign of the Norman capacity to assimilate as well as to dominate. (An account of the early Norman achievement is set out in the new museum in Bayeux where the tapestry is exhibited.) William removed most, but not all, Saxons from secular and ecclesiastical power. Despite their support for Harold, the pretender he defeated, William was able to integrate the country swiftly, as well as satisfying the hunger of his own barons.

Undoubtedly an atavistic Viking desire for plunder and glory animated the men who set sail from Dives-sur-Mer with William – a desire so strong that the conquest of England only partially fulfilled it. Since the very first years of the 11th century Normans had also been

Warfare, 1066-style, vividly depicted in the Bayeux tapestry

slipping southwards, and only five years after William had won one new kingdom the landless sons of Tancred of Hauteville near Coutances had united their compatriots in the south of Italy and won another, with the capture of Bari and Palermo in 1071. When he died in Corfu, the great Robert Guiscard was bound for Constantinople, and his son Bohemund, architect of the First Crusade ('the little god of the Christians', as the Muslims called him), was the hero of Europe on his return from Antioch in 1104. However, there was comparatively little in common between the two kingdoms, despite the marriage of Joanna, the daughter of Henry II of England and Normandy, to William II of Sicily in 1176. The couple remained childless, and the inheritance of the Normans' 'kingdom in the sun' went to the German emperor with William II's sister Constance.

Normandy Torn Between Two Crowns
The cohesion of the two lands of England and Normandy was always difficult to sustain – William Rufus, William's successor in England, had had to reconquer Normandy from his brother Robert Curthose. Despite the efforts of kings Henry II, Richard I and John, Normandy was eventually taken from the English crown – partly with the help of its own subjects – by Philip II Augustus of France. The surviving castles in Normandy mostly date from this time of conflict, the 12th century. Many were rebuilt in stone by Henry I, then strengthened during the wars of Henry II with his own sons and with Philip Augustus, or by Richard I – who founded from new the magnificent Château Gaillard on the Seine at Les Andelys – or by Philip Augustus once he had conquered Normandy from John in 1204.
Established securely as part of France by the Treaty of Paris in 1259, Normandy joined in the general peace and prosperity under St Louis IX. From this time date its wonderful cathedrals such as those of Rouen, Bayeux, Coutances, Evreux, Lisieux – rebuildings of existing churches but in the new Ile-de-France style of Gothic. Fine though they are, however, they did not make an original contribution to the development of the Gothic style.

In the mid-14th century peace was shattered by the outbreak of the Hundred Years War, as Edward III of England claimed the French crown in 1337, and by the onset of the Black Death in 1348. For Normandy, one of the main theatres of war, this was a period of decline. Still worse was to come after the spectacular successes of Henry V, landing at Harfleur and fighting his way to a brilliant victory at Agincourt in Picardy in 1415. The two crowns were jointly settled on the infant Henry VI, and the English held Normandy, with their capital at Rouen, for the next 35 years, despite the preference of most of its people for France. Joan of Arc, the Maid of Orléans, appeared on the scene in 1428. Having persuaded the French pretender, Charles, to trust in her, she rallied the French troops and drove off the English from besieged Orléans in 1429. Further victories in the Loire Valley followed, and under their impetus Charles was crowned Charles VII at Reims. In the following year Joan was captured; she was brought to Rouen and there tried as a witch, on the two main charges of having incorrect visions and wearing male clothes. She was burnt at the stake in the Vieux Marché in Rouen in May 1431. But it did the English little good. After desultory war, the French quite suddenly rolled up the English possessions in mainland France in the years 1448 to 1450, while Henry VI's madness in 1453 and the outbreak of the Wars of the Roses in 1455 prevented any English retaliation.

The Maid of Orléans – an Italian representation

The Age of the *Armateurs*

The departure of the English heralded a new era of enterprise and prosperity for Normandy, especially for its seafaring ports. Mariners from Dieppe had already reached Africa, in the wake of the Portuguese, in the late 14th century, and in the early 16th century, led by the *armateur* Jehan d'Ango, French privateers waged successful war against these rivals. Another such *armateur*, or builder and owner of privateering ships, was Jean Le Pelletier of Rouen. Like the English, these French dogs of the sea also preyed on Spanish ships, laden with the treasures of the New World, but at the same time explored in their own right: the

Florentine Verrazzano, for example, sailed
from Dieppe to discover modern Manhattan
(New York) in 1524. Such enterprise was
actively encouraged by King François I, who
founded Le Havre in 1517, and several
Normandy men had an important part to play
in affairs of state at this time, notably Georges
d'Amboise, cardinal archbishop of Rouen. The
seafaring tradition continued well into the next
century, and Honfleur had a conspicuous role
in the colonisation of French Canada, Samuel
de Champlain having sailed from its harbour to
found Québec in 1608.

Signs of Normandy's late 15th- and early 16th-
century wealth and success are abundant in its
churches and in many secular buildings as
well. Jehan d'Ango's country residence
survives at Varengeville, near Dieppe, also
Jean Le Pelletier's outside Rouen; unfortunately
Georges d'Amboise's *château* at Gaillon has
not fared so well. Numerous churches or
chapels in the late Gothic style called
Flamboyant are to be found especially in
Upper (eastern) Normandy, and number some
of the finest examples in all France. St-Maclou
in Rouen is an exceptionally large church
wholly in the Flamboyant style.

The Hundred Years War had caused an almost
total disruption in architecture, and the
Flamboyant style developed directly out of
13th-century Gothic. Already in the 13th
century the ribs of the vault and the tracery of
the windows had begun to merge to produce
an overall, harmonious effect, rendered
dazzling by colourful painting and stained
glass. But although Flamboyant was an
independent French development, it had been
anticipated by the overall 'Perpendicular' style
– its equivalent in England.

In earlier Gothic, ornament and structure are
one; in late Gothic the decoration takes over.
Although Flamboyant often seems an extreme
of the Gothic style, its decorative nature
actually made the penetration of Italian
Renaissance forms much easier. These start
appearing at the very end of the 15th century,
in the wake of the French invasions of Italy.
They were assimilated easily also because the
Italian influence came not from the heart of the

Château d'Anet

classical Renaissance, in Florence and central Italy, but from the north, around Milan, which the French ruled from 1500 to 1521, where a quite different, highly ornate, crowded style was favoured. You could say that the French simply exchanged one form of incrustation for another. Fine examples of Early Renaissance architecture are to be seen especially in the old government buildings and *hôtels* at the centre of large towns in Normandy.

However, by the middle of the 16th century a more profound change had taken place, represented by the *château* at Anet on the very eastern edge of Normandy, by Philibert de l'Orme. Indeed Anet is almost a suburb of Paris, and from this period Normandy reverted to a reflection of the styles decided by an increasingly centralised government. Not that the royal government remained indifferent to Normandy. Two initiatives by Louis XIV's minister Colbert are worth noting: the building of the Vieux Bassin harbour at Honfleur, and the establishment of a lace-working industry at Alençon. Also, Rouen and Le Havre continued to exploit their excellent trading positions, and in Rouen significant industries both in textiles and in faïence were established during the Ancien Régime.

The vernacular tradition of building in timber was not affected, even though Normandy is not short of fine *châteaux* in stone built or rebuilt over the 17th and 18th centuries. Extraordinarily enough, half-timbering has remained common up to the present day. To some this may seem artificial and false, but there is no doubt it helps to keep alive the Normandy sense of tradition – one of its strongest points.

Beaches, Railways and Aesthetes

The Revolution was not well received in conservative Normandy, where the so-called Chouan resistance continued throughout the 1790s. 'Chouan' derives from the Norman French for owl: supposedly a call imitating an owl was used as a signal by the royalist peasants. But with the 19th century there came increasingly rapid changes. The growth of Paris brought new prosperity to the farming regions of Normandy, and the development of deep-sea fishing imparted new life to its ports, notably Fécamp. At the same time certain towns and ports became favourite residences of eminent persons, for instance Louis-Philippe, who spent much time at Eu in the northeastern Bray region, and was visited there by Queen Victoria. Dieppe became a favourite haunt of English high society, despite the presence for a year or so of Oscar Wilde, who died there a social leper in 1900.

However, resort Normandy was really a product of the railways, which after the mid century rendered holiday breaks to the seaside feasible and fashionable for a much larger number of people. With its spacious beaches, pleasant breezes and atmospheric fishing ports, the Normandy coast was an ideal refuge during the hot summer months for those condemned to wear Victorian clothes. The paintings of the Honfleur artist Eugène Boudin document life and times on the promenades that began to be built, particularly along the Côte Fleurie, at that time – Cabourg is the most remarkable example of a complete Edwardian resort complex, but many other Normandy resorts still have glittering Second Empire casinos.

Above all, Normandy in this period will be known through the paintings of the Impressionists, either because, like Manet and Monet, they belonged to the class that took their family summer holidays in Normandy anyway, or because their chosen subject matter was now, with the revolution that was overtaking art, typical scenes of contemporary life – in which going to the seaside ranked high. Their own seaside still ranks high with the French, whose schools have long summer holidays that render package holidays in more exotic places impracticable. Many Parisians own houses in Normandy to which they have been coming now for generations. Modern resort Normandy has also been well documented in French films from Truffaut to Blier, and, above all, Louis Malle.

Not only the visual artists but also writers recorded the recreations of 19th-century Normandy. That does not include the sardonic

BACKGROUND

Gustave Flaubert, a native of Rouen, who instead wrote of bourgeois life inland (*Madame Bovary*), but Victor Hugo wrote a famous lament over a boating accident at Villequier on the lower Seine. At the end of the century Marcel Proust often camped in the Grand Hôtel at Cabourg, where he wrote some of *A la Récherche du Temps Perdu* (*Remembrance of Things Past*). He also created a synthetic picture of an Impressionist painter in the figure of Elstir, and depicted the new spell that Norman Romanesque architecture had begun to exert in his descriptions of 'Balbec' church.

Gustave Flaubert (1821–80)

The Battle of Normandy

During the summer of 1942, Allied military planners began to envisage the re-invasion of Europe, following the disastrous 1940 British retreat from Dunkirk. An important preliminary to the D-Day invasion on 6 June 1944 was an unsuccessful commando raid on Dieppe and nearby points in August 1942. This convinced the masterminds of 'Operation Overlord' that it would be costly, if not futile, to attempt to capture any existing port.

It was decided to opt for a beach landing, which would be supported by artificial harbours (the so-called Mulberry harbours), towed out and anchored behind the invasion force. Normandy's flat, sandy beaches were ideal for the purpose. Much of the purpose-built new technology worked well, though subsequent fighting was hard. Of course, there were mistakes and tragedies, as the numerous cemeteries reveal, but the Allies managed in many cases to land without heavy loss.

Damage to the towns and villages of Normandy was substantial, however, and the ravages of the Invasion are still evident in the many places that were gutted of their historic buildings. Reparation was not always attempted, and resulted in some eyesores.

Many museums of the Invasion are to be found in Caen, Bayeux and at many sites along the coast. Their dioramas, films, photographs and military memorabilia tell a story that, not only for present grandparents, remains a vivid chapter in Normandy's history.

What to See

The Essential rating system:

✓	'top ten' sights

◆◆◆ do not miss
◆◆ see if you can
◆ worth seeing if
you have time

NORTHEAST NORMANDY: THE PAYS DE CAUX

Strange though it may seem, the Pays de Caux was historically a rather isolated region. This northeastern area of Normandy – now corresponding broadly with the *département* of Seine-Maritime – is cut off from the rest of Normandy by the lower Seine, which used to be unbridgeable beyond Rouen.

The fertile Pays de Caux was first developed during the 19th century, when its agriculture geared up to feed Paris's expanding population, and when Le Havre, at the mouth of the Seine, grew into a major transatlantic port. Apart from Rouen, which links the two halves of Upper (eastern) Normandy, it has only one historic centre of any importance – the port of Dieppe. With its castle, old streets and unchanged ways, Dieppe is easily the most attractive of Normandy's Channel ports.

Most of the character of the Caux region is round its edges. Especially around Fécamp and Etretat, with its famous chalk cliffs (*caux* means chalk), it has a beautiful coastline. Between the resorts you will find some charming unspoilt nooks and coves directly adjoining open or wooded countryside. Its beaches are piled with great round pebbles, but there is sand below the high-water mark. To the south, the Pays de Caux is bounded by the lower valley of the Seine. Despite the heavy presence of industry here, there are woods and forests and inspiring ruins such as Jumièges, one of many important abbeys that flourished in Normandy from the 11th century. Several of them are linked together by the *Route des Abbayes* – one of 20 or so *routes touristiques* in various parts of Normandy. You will see signposts for these special-interest routes, such as the *Route des Marais* (marshes) and the *Route du Cidre*, as you travel around the region. Others to follow in Seine-Maritime include the *Route des Ivoirés et des Epices* (ivory and spices) around Dieppe, the *Route des Colombiers* (dovecotes) and a *Route des*

Fromages, which explores the cheese country around Neufchâtel-en-Bray.

On its eastern side, the Caux region has a number of old forests that follow the line of river valleys, providing views and variety for walkers, cyclists and picnickers. Examples are the Forêt d'Eu along the River Bresle (which separates Normandy from Picardy), and the Forêt d'Eawy (pronounced 'ee-a-vi') along the River Varenne south of Dieppe. The Eawy forest adjoins the northern point of the charming Bray region, famous for its cheese and apples. Here there are many timber-framed houses and barns (known as *chaumières*) set among orchards – a similar landscape to that of the flat parts of the lower Seine Valley. Some of the farms where cheese is made are open for visits or tasting – definitely a bonus as you tour this attractive region. Classic local cheeses include Neufchâtel, Gournay and Petit-Suisse.

In the centre of the Caux plateau, towns like Yvetot and Tôtes are scarcely more than built-up crossroads. There is little to see out of the window as you travel, only open and flat arable countryside. Perhaps for this reason, many British visitors arriving at Le Havre miss this part of Normandy by using the great toll-bridge – the Pont de Tancarville – near the mouth of the Seine. However, it can be just as convenient to stay north of the Seine and cross by the Pont de Brotonne or, further east, at Rouen.

WHAT TO SEE

ARQUES-LA-BATAILLE
southwest of Dieppe

The **castle** at Arques was one of the great early castles of Normandy, on a classic hilltop site overlooking the confluence of the rivers Béthune and Varenne. Abandoned in the 17th century, it is now all ruins. The typically Anglo-Norman square keep and the bailey are due to Henry I, who took it over in 1123. The entrance was refortified in the 16th century, and its four larger towers were built to house cannon.
Open: at all times.

The village takes the 'Bataille' (battle) part of its name from the victory won here in 1589 by Henry of Navarre. As a result he became Henri IV of France and settled the Huguenot Wars which had divided the kingdom. A monument marks the site.

◆◆
CANY, CHÂTEAU DE
east of Fécamp
This fine château, built between 1640 and 1646 and attributed to the royal architect François Mansart, is wonderfully enhanced by its superb setting. A stately approach between service blocks is set off by a series of moats and canals fed from the nearby River Derdent. The château is surrounded by a park that was landscaped *à l'anglaise* in the early 19th century. The main house, reached by an elegantly curved double staircase, preserves much of its original 17th-century furniture, woodwork and decoration.
Open: Saturday to Thursday, July and August.
Closed: 4th Sunday in July.

◆
CAUDEBEC-EN-CAUX
on the Seine, south of Yvetot
A small town with views out from its cliff over the Seine on to the **Forêt de Brotonne**, Caudebec sits beside the newly built **Pont de Brotonne** (toll). Most traffic whistles past Caudebec up to Yvetot or down to the Seine valley floor without stopping, but Caudebec was once a more important place and is well worth a visit.
Its church of **Notre-Dame**, dominating the market square, is a fine example of the Flamboyant Gothic style, in which the region of Normandy is so rich. Look closely at the stained glass, as well as the tracery. There are also statues taken from the nearby great abbey of Jumièges (see page 28).
The so-called **Maison des Templars** near the church dates from the 13th century. Another beautiful Flamboyant church, dated 1519, lies just north of Caudebec at **Ste-Gertrude**, on the D40.

Castle ruins, Arques-la-Bataille

Accommodation and Restaurants

Caudebec is also worth visiting for a meal. Try the highly acclaimed new restaurant in the **Manoir de Rétival** hotel, rue St Clair (tel: 35 96 11 22) or the established **Normandie**, 19 quai Guilbaud (tel: 35 96 25 11).

Tourist Office

Hôtel de Ville, place Charles de Gaulle (tel: 35 96 20 65).

◆

CLÈRES

north of Rouen

The park of the château at Clères was landscaped in the 19th century, and since 1920 has been a **parc zoologique**.

Here you can see exotic birds (such as flamingos, cranes and ornamental ducks), antelopes, kangaroos, emus and monkeys. Clères offers not theme-park thrills, but an old-fashioned 'paradise' in a woodland setting. The château is a pretty 19th-century Gothic revival building on an ancient site.
Open: daily, Easter to August; weekends in spring and autumn.

Also at Clères is the **Musée d'automobiles de Normandie** (Normandy Car Museum). The collection includes several very early cars, as well as military vehicles of World War II and a diorama of the 1944 invasion.
Open: daily, all year.

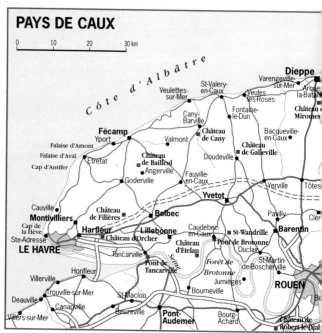

PAYS DE CAUX

◆◆◆
DIEPPE

Dieppe still uses its typically
Norman river-mouth **harbour**, a
long thin slit between the cliffs
which penetrates right into the
town dwarfing the rooftops,
although the ferry from
Newhaven in England no longer
threads its gigantic way along it.
A new port beside the eastern
cliff makes arrival and departure
much easier for cars and lorries,
leaving the pleasant town itself
undisturbed by periodic
blockages. Dieppe has a long,
flat pebble **beach** on an
esplanade currently occupied
for much of August by an
enormous funfair. The town
itself is mostly a warren of small

The port and waterfront at Dieppe

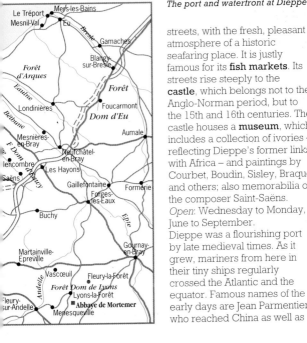

streets, with the fresh, pleasant
atmosphere of a historic
seafaring place. It is justly
famous for its **fish markets**. Its
streets rise steeply to the
castle, which belongs not to the
Anglo-Norman period, but to
the 15th and 16th centuries. The
castle houses a **museum**, which
includes a collection of ivories –
reflecting Dieppe's former links
with Africa – and paintings by
Courbet, Boudin, Sisley, Braque
and others; also memorabilia of
the composer Saint-Saëns.
Open: Wednesday to Monday,
June to September.
Dieppe was a flourishing port
by late medieval times. As it
grew, mariners from here in
their tiny ships regularly
crossed the Atlantic and the
equator. Famous names of the
early days are Jean Parmentier,
who reached China as well as

America, Jean Denis, who got to Brazil, the Florentine Verrazzano who sailed from here to land for the first time on the future site of New York, and also Jean Fleury who captured the Spanish bullion fleet returning from Mexico in 1521. A famous Dieppe citizen was the *armateur* or privateer magnate Jehan (Jean or John) Ango who, in the early 16th century, built and equipped a series of squadrons which successfully attacked the Portuguese and Spanish in the seas around Africa and America. Ango became rich enough to ransom his king, François I, after his capture by Charles V in 1525. He is buried in **St-Jacques**, the main church of Dieppe, which also contains other mementoes of the town's seafaring heyday. During World War II, Dieppe was the object of what Churchill called a 'reconnaissance in depth' in August 1942, when several thousand Allied troops, including many Canadians, landed and suffered heavy losses. This 'Operation Jubilee' demonstrated how well defended the Channel ports were, and the Allies made no further attempts to recapture existing harbours. The lessons learnt were important for D-Day strategy two years later.
The best **beaches** are to the west of Dieppe. Inland, off the Paris road, is the **Forêt d'Eawy**, along the valley of the Varenne; the D154 to Bellencombre and St-Saëns is a pretty drive, and the forest tracks are good for walking and cycling. A fire-break, the Allée des Limousins,

cleaves the length of the forest. Originally the Eawy joined up with the similar Forêt de Lyons further south.

Accommodation
The main hotels are along the boulevard Verdun, facing the beach: the moderately expensive **La Présidence**, 1 boulevard Verdun (tel: 35 84 31 31) with an upstairs seaview restaurant; the more modest **Hotel de la Plage** (tel: 35 84 18 28) or **Epsom** (tel: 35 84 10 18), further down the same boulevard, without restaurants. There are cheaper ones in the streets behind.

Restaurants
Dieppe boasts some good fish restaurants, for example **La Mélie**, 2 Grande rue du Pollet, located in the fishermen's quarter (tel: 35 84 21 19), or the **Marmite Dieppoise**, 8 rue St-Jean (just by the church of St-Jacques, tel: 35 84 24 26). Others are on the quai Henri IV, the street along the western side of the harbour.

Tourist Office
1 boulevard du Général de Gaulle (tel: 35 84 11 77).

◆

ETELAN, CHÂTEAU D'
near Norville, southeast of Lillebonne
To match its Flamboyant Gothic churches, Normandy has some excellent surviving secular buildings of the same period. This historic château is a beautiful example, with its bands of red brick and white stone, and its exquisite weathered pinnacles, some of which adorn a grand external

staircase on three storeys.
Open: Wednesday to Monday
afternoons, mid-July to August.

◆◆
ETRETAT

Etretat is a classic family-
holiday place in the delightful
Norman tradition. Dead in
winter, it is packed with visitors
of every nationality in summer,
when parking is an
achievement. You may have to
go at least as far out as the
church of **Notre-Dame**, east of
the town centre. This sizeable
Romanesque building was
rendered even more
Romanesque in the 19th
century.

The town itself is small, full of
timber-framed buildings
creaking with not terribly old
antiquity. Etretat's happy
atmosphere is its best quality.
There is a typical beach
promenade and pebble beach,
set off by two great cliffs at each
end, one of which has split away
spectacularly to form one
detached 'needle' (*L'Aiguille*)
with another still clinging. There
are walks from the town up both
cliffs, but the path becomes a
human ant-stream in August.
There is a famous painting of
one of the cliffs by Seurat, and
several other Impressionists
also painted here.

Etretat is the prettiest resort of
the so-called **Côte d'Albâtre**
(Alabaster Coast). But the coves
and beaches between Etretat
and Fécamp – some accessible
only on foot – are also
charming, and quieter. The
town has a few central hotels,
such as the **Falaises**, boulevard
Coty (tel: 35 27 02 77). There

The Falaise d'Aval, near Etretat

are also a couple of reasonably
good restaurants on the
promenade, including **Roches
Blanches**, terrasse Eugène
Boudin (tel: 35 27 07 34). But
there is not a wide choice.

Tourist Office
Hôtel de Ville (tel: 35 27 05 21).

◆
EU

Eu is an historic town (only just
in Normandy), much dwindled
from its former importance,
when William the (future)
Conqueror was married here in
1050. Its centrepiece is the
church of **Notre-Dame et St-
Laurent**, a High Gothic building
with some fine 15th-century
fitments and tombs, including
one of the St Lawrence to whom
it is dedicated – actually an Irish
saint, St Lawrence O'Toole, who
died at Eu in the 12th century.

The château has a late 16th-century Renaissance core, but was entirely refitted when it became one of the French royal pretender Louis-Philippe's favourite residences. He received Queen Victoria here in 1843 and 1845. Unfortunately fire later gutted the interior, and though the building houses the **Musée Louis-Philippe**, it has virtually no decoration dating from his time.
Open: Wednesday to Monday, Easter to October.
Inland the **Forêt d'Eu**, following the line of the River Bresle, is broken up by several large open clearings. There are paths for walking and cycling.

Tourist Office
41 rue Bignon (tel: 35 86 04 68).

FÉCAMP
Until recently Fécamp was a leading fishing port, specialising in deep-sea cod-fishing; its harbour has now become more of a yacht marina. The **beach** here is typical of the Caux coast, wide, bare and pebbly. The town lacks the character and atmosphere of nearby Etretat, but it is larger and not so exclusively a resort.
Fécamp was the home of one of the greatest of Normandy's famous Benedictine monasteries. Its origins go back to the 7th century, and its early 11th-century abbot, William of Volpiano, was one of the leading churchmen of his age. The enormous abbey church of **La Trinité** has traces of Romanesque here and there. Mostly, however, it is a High Gothic building, much altered, especially in the 18th century. Politely you might call it dignified and majestic; impolitely, vast and dull.
The **Musée de la Bénédictine** is best known as a museum of the well-known Bénédictine liqueur, but has other memorabilia of the monastery where the liqueur was first made in the 16th century.
Open: daily, all year.
Fécamp's **Musée Centre-des-Arts** has a small collection of 19th-century paintings and obsolete items of local craft and industry. Facing the sea, the **Musée des Terre-Nuevas et de la Pêche** revives Fécamp's prestigious maritime past through boats, models, tools and paintings.
Open: both museums Wednesday to Monday.
Closed: major public holidays.

Accommodation and Restaurants
A pleasant small hotel, also a restaurant, is the **Auberge de la Rouge**, just inland at St-Léonard on the D925 to Le Havre (tel: 35 28 07 59). There are good fish restaurants by the harbour, for example the unpretentious **L'Escalier**, 101 quai Bérigny (tel: 35 28 26 79).

Tourist Office
113 rue Alexandre le Grand (tel: 35 28 51 01).

FILIÈRES, CHÂTEAU DE
off the N15 from Le Havre, near Gommerville
This splendid, if understated neoclassical château of the late 18th century is attributed to the

Fécamp's Musée de la Benedictine

architect Victor Louis. It was an incomplete rebuilding of a 16th-century château, of which one wing remains. Its park setting and precious but severe interiors are its main features.
Open: afternoons daily, July and August; Wednesday, weekends and holidays, Easter to June and September to October.

◆

HAVRE, LE

Said to be Europe's third largest port, Le Havre is chiefly about oil: a bank of shiny refineries stretches from its harbour for several miles up the north bank of the Seine. It is also a ferry port, with links to Portsmouth as well as to Rosslare and Cork in Ireland. This is what brings most visitors to Le Havre today. The town was once a popular centre for sailing and family holidays (a big regatta is still held in July), but it was bombed flat in the War. Though rebuilt according to modern principles under the aegis of the distinguished architect Auguste Perret, Le

Havre is now a soulless place, lacking the charm that might tempt visitors to linger. Numerous main roads lead here, nonetheless. Le Havre has a special link to the Paris-Caen motorway by the arching **Pont de Tancarville** (toll) and by another bridge due for completion in 1994 which will come out close to Honfleur. Reminders of old Le Havre can be seen in two museums. One – the **Musée de l'Ancien Havre** – recreates the town from its foundation in 1517. The other – the **Musée des Beaux-Arts André Malraux** – is one of the best museums in Normandy. It is devoted chiefly to the paintings of Raoul Dufy and Eugène Boudin , whose strong, delicate pictures are on show here in their full variety (see also page 54).
Open: both museums Wednesday to Monday.
Closed: major holidays.
Just west of Le Havre, **Ste-Adresse** – once a fashionable

summer residence – is a name
that features in Impressionist
painting. Today it has little
atmosphere even as a village.
There is, however, a beach
(with even more pebbles than
most on the Caux coast), used
mostly by locals. Further north,
the coast is inaccessible (partly
because of a second port for
tankers at Le Havre–Antifer)
until you come to Etretat.

To the east, **Harfleur** is an older
port than Le Havre: it features in
Shakespeare's *Henry V*. Though
engulfed by its neighbour, it has
just kept its identity. Further east
still is the **Château d'Orcher**,
which Henry V gave to Sir John
Falstolf, the formidable soldier
on whom Shakespeare's Falstaff
was based.

Open: afternoons daily, July to
mid-August.

Accommodation

The two major hotels are the
Bordeaux, 147 rue Brindeau
(tel: 35 22 69 44), and the
Mercure (one of the chain),
chaussée d'Angoulême (tel: 35
19 55 55). There are several
more in the Quartier Moderne,
south of avenue Foch.

Restaurants

The classy restaurants are at **Ste-
Adresse,** for instance **Beau
Séjour,** 3 place Clemenceau (tel:
35 46 19 69), **Nice-Havrais,
Yves Page** – it is not easy to
choose between them. Good,
traditional fare is available in Le
Havre itself at **L'Athanor,** 120 rue
Guillemard (tel: 35 42 50 27).

Tourist Office

1 place de l'Hôtel de Ville
(tel: 35 21 22 88).

♦♦♦
JUMIÈGES ✓

*on the north bank of the Seine,
west of Rouen; also accessible by
ferry from Port-Jumièges on the
south bank*

On a flat peninsula jutting into
the winding Seine, Jumièges is
one of the most beautiful empty
choirs in a land rich in ruined
abbeys. The west end of the
church (**Notre-Dame**) still rises
to its full height, but the nave is
roofless and the east end razed
(it was used as a quarry after the
Revolution). There are also
substantial remains of the
monastic buildings.

The church is early
Romanesque in style: it was
consecrated in 1067, well
before the great Abbaye aux
Hommes at Caen (see page 57).
The west end has an upstairs
chapel over the porch, between
flanking towers, and the nave,
once roofed in timber, was
braced by stone arches across
every other bay. The nave
opened into a crossing over
which there rose a tower, and a
chancel with an ambulatory.
This, however, was enlarged in
the Gothic period.

From the choir there is a
passage into a second, older
church, **St-Pierre,** which had
been outgrown by the abbey;
there are 10th-century parts at
the west end. The **chapter
house** is of the early 12th
century – its later date shows in
its slightly pointed arches. A
gnarled yew stands in the
former cloister, and pleasant
grounds surround the ruins.

Open: Wednesday to Monday.
Closed: major holidays.

The abbey at Jumièges

LE HAVRE see HAVRE, LE

LE TRÉPORT see TRÉPORT, LE

LILLEBONNE

Today a satellite of Le Havre to the west, in Roman times Lillebonne was the major port at the mouth of the Seine. The considerable **amphitheatre** of the former Juliobona, dating from the 1st and 2nd centuries AD, has been excavated.
Open: Friday to Wednesday. Key available at café near Hôtel de Ville.

Tourist Office
4 rue Pasteur (tel: 35 38 08 45).

MARTAINVILLE
east of Rouen
Privateer or *armateur* Jacques Le Pelletier of Rouen built the château here about 1481. It was originally a square, moated castle with four round towers. Some 30 years later, the castle was remodelled by Le Pelletier's nephew, who dismantled the battlements,

built the present steep roofs and replaced the tiny windows with large ones. He also filled in the moat, ripping out the drawbridge and introducing the present portal and beautiful Flamboyant Gothic bay window above it. Not neglecting defence altogether, he protected the house with a wall with four towers (three survive). This was not to guard against siege from an army, but to prevent robbery by marauding bands – a serious problem in the late Middle Ages.
This castle, almost untouched, was bought by the state in 1960. It now houses a collection of Normandy furniture and utensils.
Open: Wednesday to Monday. *Closed*: major holidays.

MESNIÈRES EN BRAY
northwest of Neufchâtel-en-Bray
The château here is one of the few in Normandy to rival those of the Loire – at least, those of

the same date. Situated on the River Béthune, it was started about 1500 and finished about 1546 by the powerful Boissay family. It consists of a square block with four massive round towers at the corners. The central courtyard was opened up on the river side in the early 18th century, and a previously hidden Italianate loggia now forms the central feature of the garden front. The interior is known for unusual 17th-century wooden statues of stags.
Open: guided visits only, Saturday and Sunday afternoons, April to October.

◆

MIROMESNIL, CHÂTEAU DE
south of Dieppe
Built in a superb baroque style of the mid-17th century, the château is famous as the birthplace of the brilliant writer of short stories Guy de Maupassant – friend of Zola and Proust – and has memorabilia of him. A 16th-century chapel survives from the château's predecessor on the site.
Open: Wednesday to Monday afternoons, May to mid-October.

◆

ST-MARTIN-DE-BOSCHERVILLE
beside the Seine west of Rouen
The former 11th-century abbey here became a parish church – **St-Georges** – at the time of the Revolution, and so avoided destruction. It is a solid example of mature Norman Romanesque, datable between 1080 and 1125, except for the 13th-century vaults. It has some figurative capitals, though many have been mutilated.

◆

ST-VALÉRY-EN-CAUX
With its two flanking cliffs, St-Valéry is sometimes regarded as a smaller version of Etretat. However, it has more of a harbour – now full of yachts rather than fishing smacks – and less of a beach.

The harbour, St-Valéry-en-Caux

Accommodation
The hotel **Les Terrasses**, 22 rue
Le Perrey (tel: 35 97 11 22), is
right on the beach.

Restaurants
Two good restaurants for fish
are the **Port**, on the harbour
(tel: 35 97 08 93), and the
Pigeon-Blanc, by the old
church (tel: 35 97 90 22).

Tourist Office
place Hôtel de Ville (tel: 35 97
00 63).

ST-WANDRILLE
east of Caudebec-en-Caux
The **abbey** of St-Wandrille is
an historic and holy site. Its
monastic origins lie in the 7th
century, and though the
ancient buildings have long
been in ruins, the abbey has
been refounded. Today, the
monks' services are held in a
vast but starkly beautiful
medieval barn, painstakingly
transported here piece by
piece from its original site and
rebuilt.
The old church at St-Wandrille
consists only of stumps, but the
cloister, dating from the 14th
and 15th centuries, has
survived better. Not far away,
the chapel of **St-Saturnin** is
heavily restored, but its trefoil
plan probably goes back at
least to the 8th century.
Open: guided visits only,
Monday to Saturday afternoons,
Sunday and feast-day
mornings.

Restaurant
The **Auberge Deux Couronnes**
is a good restaurant opposite
the abbey (tel: 35 96 11 44).

TRÉPORT, LE
This most easterly of
Normandy's resorts is much
frequented by Parisians in
summer. Today much less chic
than Deauville, it was an
extremely fashionable resort
more than 100 years ago, when
Louis-Philippe used to reside at
nearby Eu (see page 25). Like
Deauville, Le Tréport has a
quieter sister the other side of
the river-mouth harbour –
Mers-les-Bains. There are
reasonable fish restaurants
along the harbour quay.

Tourist Office
esplanade de la Plage (tel: 35
86 05 69).

VALMONT
east of Fécamp
The castle, church and town
here were once the property
of the d'Estouteville family,
first recorded in the 9th
century, who later followed
William across the Channel
and did well from the
Conquest. Of the **abbey** only
the Chapelle de la Vierge
(Lady Chapel) and some other
parts of the east end remain
standing, though they are
flanked by remaining
buildings dating from the
monastery's revival in the 17th
century. The chapel still has
some fine 16th-century fittings
and sculpture inside.
Open: Wednesday to Monday,
April to September.
Closed: 15 August.
The **castle** has a great Norman
keep with an incongruous steep
tiled roof, added to match the
rest of the château that was

built on to it, one part in the 15th century and the rest in the mid-16th century. Unfortunately this Renaissance wing was spoilt by a 19th-century restoration, though the arcades of the loggia survive.

Open: afternoons daily, July and August; Saturdays and Sundays only April to June and September to October.

◆
VARENGEVILLE-SUR-MER
west of Dieppe

The **Manoir d'Ango**, near this small seaside village, was built by the famous 16th-century Dieppe *armateur* Jehan Ango (see page 24) as a country house where he could retire in style and enjoy his wealth. Unfortunately the house was later badly damaged and was unfaithfully restored, but the outlines remain, as do some

A window in Varengeville church

outstanding original features, such as the large round dovecote richly decorated in terracotta and flint. Dating from 1532–44, the house is an example of the French Early Renaissance, much influenced by the Po-valley styles the French had seen on King François's campaigns in North Italy – hence the Manoir's loggia and the broad frieze running above it.

Open: daily, Easter to October; weekends and holidays in winter.

Also at Varengeville is a slice of Edwardian England, the **Parc des Moustiers**. The house was designed in 1898 by the young Edwin Lutyens (much influenced by Norman Shaw and the Arts and Crafts movement). An exquisite garden was laid out by Gertrude Jekyll. In this period Dieppe was a favourite resort for the English aristocracy.

Open: house by special arrangement only; gardens daily, Easter to October.

◆
VEULETTES-SUR-MER
between St-Valéry-en-Caux and Fécamp

This coastal resort is no more than a village on a beach that hums into life in the season, despite the new nuclear power-station round the headland. It is a pleasant place, with a good small hotel and restaurant overlooking the sea: **Les Frégates**, rue de la Plage (tel: 35 97 51 22).

Tourist Office
esplanade du Casino (tel: 35 97 51 33).

ROUEN

Rouen is where it is because it was until recently the lowest point on the Seine that could be bridged. A Roman settlement here was revived by Rollo, the Viking ruler of Normandy, in the early 9th century.

Of Rouen's early prosperity its great 13th-century cathedral is the most obvious sign, a High Gothic heaven-scraper to rival those of nearby Amiens, Beauvais or Chartres. From the 14th century it preserves among other things the belfry of the Gros Horloge (Great Clock), its most famous monument, arching over the oldest street in the city. But the later 14th century and early 15th century saw the troubles of the Hundred Years War with England. Rouen was a crucial city in Henry V's campaign to re-conquer Normandy, and once he had taken it in 1418 it remained in English hands till 1449.

It was during this low period for France that Joan of Arc entered the scene, reviving French fortunes until she was captured and taken to Rouen, where she was condemned on false charges for witchcraft and burnt at the stake in 1431. The Place du Vieux-Marché, where the deed was done, is in the very centre of the old city, but is now dominated by an incongruous modern church dedicated to her (she was made a saint in 1920).

The end of the 15th century and the beginning of the 16th were Rouen's greatest period. It was the capital of a rich region, while its merchants and fleet-owners carried their trade to the Old and New Indies (or stole the cargoes of the Spanish and Portuguese who had been there). From this period date the church of St-Maclou and

The Gros Horloge

some of Rouen's famous half-timbered houses – more than 700 in all. The grander examples include the **Palais de Justice** (see below) and the **Hôtel de Bourgtheroulde** (off the Vieux-Marché), with its fine early 16th-century courtyard. Even after this heyday Rouen remained prominent. It was the birthplace of the classical playwright Corneille and of the severe novelist Flaubert. It became industrialised rapidly, capitalising on its colonial trading links to become a textile centre in the 18th century. As a port and centre of industry it inevitably became a target during World War II, but the ravages to its architecture have

been repaired and its heavy industry once again lines the Seine. Its suburbs have spread to the river's south side and up into the heights overlooking the city from the north. The pedestrianised old city nestles among them like a pearl. Rouen has museums enough for a week of rainy days. Those worth visiting even in the sunshine are described under **What to See**, below. Others cover various aspects of Rouen's history, from Joan of Arc (**Musée Jeanne d'Arc**) to ironwork, tools and locks (**Musée le Secq des Tournelles**) and from famous local writers (**Musée Corneille** and **Musée Flaubert**) to the

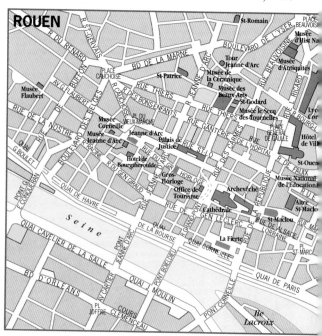

faïence industry in Rouen (**Musée de la Céramique**). One way to see the sights of Rouen is to take the 'tourist train', which leaves the place de la Cathédrale on regular narrated tours in summer.

WHAT TO SEE

◆◆
CATHEDRAL

Rouen Cathedral was begun in 1145, just after Notre-Dame in Paris and Chartres, just before Amiens, Beauvais and Reims. However, it is not so well known as those because it represents no particular advance in the steady development of Gothic architecture during those years.

Its four levels or storeys are rather clumsy compared to the normal three, breaking up the vertical lines, and it lacks the breathtaking simplicity of Chartres or Amiens. That does not mean it is not impressive. It has the tallest medieval crossing tower in France. It has a rich heritage of sculpture and stone-carving, inside and out, of the 14th, 15th and 16th centuries. This includes especially its northern portal (Portail des Libraires) and the tombs in the chancel, one of them holding the heart of King Richard the Lionheart. Those in the Lady Chapel are some of the most ornate and splendid tombs of the French Renaissance. There is also good stained glass, mostly of the 13th to 16th centuries. Clodion's Christ, on the main altar, is a fine 18th-century work.
Circulation is restricted during services

◆◆
MUSÉE DES BEAUX-ARTS

rue Thiers, beside place Vendreul, on the north side of the old city
Here you will find a small international collection of Old Masters and a larger one of French paintings (including works by Poussin, Champaigne and Géricault). Naturally the museum also houses works by Impressionists, but only one of Monet's famous series of pictures of the façade of Rouen Cathedral.
Open: Wednesday afternoon to Monday.
Closed: some holidays.

The remarkable Aître St-Maclou, a 16th-century cemetery

◆
MUSÉE DES ANTIQUITÉS DE LA SEINE MARITIME
198 Rue Beauvoisine, at the bottom of the hill where the N1 heads north to Dieppe
A comprehensive array of objects on display here documents the area's rich Roman and medieval history.
Open: Wednesday to Monday.
Closed: holidays.

◆◆
OLD CITY
centres on rue du Gros-Horloge
The old city is just about a walkable proposition: go down from the Vieux Marché along the rue du Gros-Horloge to the Cathedral and behind it St-Maclou (see below). Then walk up to the outstanding 14th- and 15th-century church of **St-Ouen** and back again along the Ganterie or rue Thiers (with the Musée des Beaux-Arts). In this square there are numerous streets with old timber-framed houses, as well as the major churches, and also smart shopping streets such as the Ganterie.

◆◆
PALAIS DE JUSTICE
rue du Gros-Horloge
Apart from houses, Rouen has several timber-framed buildings described as palaces or *hôtels*. The grandest – also incorporating stonework – is the Palais de Justice (Law Courts), a government building of the 16th century. The old belfry adjoining the Gros Horloge can be entered by a staircase of 1457, and houses a small museum of old clocks. From the top there is a view of the city.
Open: Wednesday afternoon to Monday, Easter to early October.

◆◆◆
ST-MACLOU ✓

behind cathedral

In all France there is no finer piece of late Flamboyant Gothic architecture than this. Large churches wholly in this style are rare; Flamboyant appears mostly in chapels and by way of addition and repair to existing churches. In St-Maclou, despite a long building period (1437–1517), the slender, gently twining tracery ('flame-like' – hence the name) lends great homogeneity to the church. The organ dates from the same period as the building (1521), as does the Aître St-Maclou (St-Maclou Cemetery) close by. This is another rarity: virtually all such cemeteries were built over after the Revolution. A few figures of a Dance of Death survive on the columns supporting the 16th-century houses.

Accommodation

Rouen's grand old hotel is the **Dieppe** with its **Quatre Saisons** restaurant, place Tissot (tel: 35 71 96 00), but there are some other comfortable hotels both in the centre (**Le Dandy**, 93 rue Cauchoise, tel: 35 07 32 00) and south of the river by the Parc des Expositions. Otherwise there are several small, reasonably priced hotels in the old city. Two with parking are the **Québec**, 18–24 rue Québec (tel: 35 70 09 38) and the **Viking**, 21 quai du Havre (tel: 35 70 34 95).

Restaurants

Rouen has its fair share of smart, expensive restaurants,

Flamboyant Gothic – a Style for France

The ornate late Gothic style of architecture known as 'Flamboyant' is particularly associated with Normandy. Flamboyant derives from the flame-like tracery of the windows – though it tends to invade portals, porches and ceilings too. The decoration is almost an end in itself, taking over and masking the structure. Many churches and chapels in Normandy show, in part at least, the exuberance and richness of Flamboyant Gothic.

However, St-Maclou is one of few large churches entirely in this style. This is partly for historical reasons.

Flamboyant developed, as an independent French style, after the end of the Hundred Years War.

The century of intermittent conflict had halted architectural development, but the late 15th century was a period of relative peace and prosperity. The great cathedrals were already built, so the new style was used for personal projects such as tombs, chantry chapels, and other additions or embellish-ments to existing buildings. Rouen Cathedral has a splendid array of tombs, and a chapel in the Flamboyant style was added to Lisieux Cathedral by the 15th-century bishop Pierre Cauchon. Churches in the Flamboyant style can be seen at Caudebec-en-Caux, Alençon and Verneuil-sur-Avre.

offering both old-time
Normandy favourites in cream
sauces and modern cuisine.
Gill (in the second category) is
the top, 9 quai Bourse (tel: 35 71
16 14). Less pretentious and
expensive but also outstanding
is the **Beffroy**, 15 rue Beffroy
(tel: 35 71 55 27). Both these are
closed for part of the high
season. A close third is the
Auberge du Vieux Carré, 34
rue Ganterie (tel: 35 71 67 70).
Besides these, in the old city
you will find both tourist-traps –

Rouen has plenty of restaurants

for example, Rouen's most
famous restaurant, **La Couronne**,
31 place du Vieux-Marché (tel:
35 71 40 90) – and excellent,
reasonable places, for
example, **Les Maraîchers**, 37
place du Vieux-Marché (tel: 35
71 57 73), or **Les Halles du
Vieux-Marché**, 41 place du
Vieux-Marché (tel: 35 71 03 58).

Tourist Office
25 place de la Cathédrale
(tel: 32 08 32 40).

THE SEINE VALLEY

The region of Normandy between Rouen and Paris, along and around the valley of the Seine, seems to belong to a different category from the rest, being a long way from the sea and adjacent to Paris's suburbs. One of this region's most famous sights – Monet's garden at Giverny – is just the outermost of several places down the Seine from Paris where the Impressionists used to paint. The great ducal forest at Lyons-la-Forêt is comparable to that at Fontainebleau, south of Paris (though, as it happens, the French king never built a palace here). The châteaux at Anet and Bizy were not so much country houses as refuges from the capital a little beyond Versailles.

In the Middle Ages this was border country. The splendid Château Gaillard, on the Seine above Les Andelys, was built by Richard the Lionheart to hold the border between Normandy and the Ile de France. The modern boundary is nearer to Paris at Vernon.

Today, much of the Seine Valley is heavily built up, and its sights and amenities are well known and well used by the residents

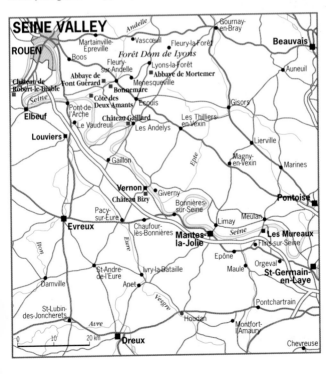

THE SEINE VALLEY

of nearby Paris. But although the proximity of Paris makes itself felt here, there are still patches of authentic Normandy. You will still find towns and villages with half-timbered houses and a rural atmosphere. Tracts of forest, a scattering of small châteaux and traditional farmsteads make it hard to forget that, despite the commuter age, this is still Normandy.

WHAT TO SEE

♦♦♦
ANDELYS, LES ✓

Beneath Richard the Lionheart's superbly sited Château Gaillard high above the winding Seine lie the merged twin villages of Petit Andely and Grand Andely. The old buildings of Petit Andely nestle below the castle on the banks of the Seine, where a riverside walk offers stunning views. Nearby, a

Château Gaillard and the Seine

typically French tree-lined square is overlooked by the simple 12th-century church of **St-Sauveur**.

Grand Andely has an altogether different feel, busier and more modern. Its square has a good **market**, and its church – **Notre-Dame** – is large and impressive. Visit Grand Andely for shopping and banks, but stay in Petit Andely – and visit the castle even if you don't like castles, for you are unlikely to find a better view of the Seine Valley.

Château Gaillard itself remains one of the best preserved and most interesting castles of its period. '*Qu' elle est belle, ma fille d'un an!*' (My lovely year-old daughter!), Richard the Lionheart is said to have exclaimed in 1197 as he saw the newly founded castle rise on its rock. Unfortunately Château Gaillard was taken by Philip Augustus in a night assault only seven years later. Philip's troops, entering through the conduits for the latrines in the towers, caught the defenders before they had time to scramble back into the keep.

Both Richard and Philip were professional soldier kings whose new castles were the technological masterpieces of their era. This one has been maintained but not modernised, so although some of the outer defences are gone, it is easy to see the original plan. Château Gaillard had four layers of defence: first the triangular *châtelet* protects the approach to the bailey walls; then within the bailey walls a *chemise*

swelling with closely set towers rings the last refuge, the keep. *Open*: keep, Wednesday afternoon to Monday, mid-March to mid-November. Free access to the bailey.

Accommodation and Restaurants

The hotel-restaurant **Chaine d'Or**, 27 rue Grande (tel: 32 54 00 31), is a popular and attractively sited old inn. A runner-up, less expensive, is the nearby **Normandie**, 1 rue Grande (tel: 32 54 10 52.)

Tourist Office

24 rue Philippe-Auguste (tel: 32 54 41 93).

ANET, CHÂTEAU D'
on the River Eure, southeast of Evreux

The château at Anet, built for Diane de Poitiers, mistress of Henri II, during the 1540s and 1550s, is the most important surviving work by the hugely influential Philibert de l'Orme, the founding father of French classicism.

Though much of the château is no longer, his remarkable entrance gateway and chapel survive. The entrance is bold, massive and monumental, and represents the earliest attempt in France to reproduce fortress-like grandeur in the language of classical architecture. The chapel was the first French church with a centralised (rather than longitudinal) plan – inspired by Italian Renaissance architecture. Philibert evolved a complex scheme involving advanced geometry, producing a dizzying effect when you

The west front of Evreux Cathedral

enter beneath the dome.
Open: afternoons Wednesday to Monday, April to October; also Sunday and holiday mornings; Saturday, Sunday and holiday afternoons all year.

◆
BIZY, CHÂTEAU DE
on the southwestern edge of Vernon
Much of this once outstanding 18th-century château was destroyed after the Revolution, but it was rebuilt and refurbished in the 19th century. The outbuildings, including magnificent stables (now housing a collection of vintage cars) go back to the days of the château's original glory, when it was the scene of lavish fêtes put on by the fabulously wealthy duc de Belle-Isle. The grand avenues of lime trees are 18th-century, but the rest of the park was redesigned *à l'anglaise* in the 19th century.
Open: Saturday to Thursday, April to October.

◆
ECOUIS
north of Les Andelys
The village of Ecouis marks the centre of the so-called **Vexin normand**, a region of fields and forests on the north bank of the Seine southeast of Rouen. Ecouis is known for its twin-towered 14th-century **church**, endowed by the local Marigny family. Inside is a remarkable collection of painted wooden sculptures of the same period.

◆◆
EVREUX
Evreux might be thought of as a smaller version of Rouen. This pleasant and historic country town is set on the little River Iton – the walk along the old ramparts by the river is one of the town's best features.
The **cathedral**, smaller than Rouen's though ambitious, has had its 12th-century core patched, rebuilt or improved many times as a result of repeated war damage all through Evreux's strife-torn history. The museum in the nearby **Ancien Evêché**

(Bishop's Palace) has a limited collection, though its archaeology section is extensive.
Open: Tuesday to Sunday.
Closed: Sunday mornings and holidays.
Like Rouen, Evreux has an historic clock, but for dedicated medievalists the town's outstanding treasure is the precious 13th-century reliquary of Louis XI in the pretty church of **St-Taurin**, a local bishop saint.

Accommodation and Restaurants

There is quite a wide choice of hotel-restaurants, from the modernised and rather expensive **France**, a restaurant-with-rooms overlooking the river at 29 rue St-Thomas (tel: 32 39 09 25), to the old-world **Normandy**, 37 rue Feray (tel: 32 33 14 40).

Tourist Office

1 place Général de Gaulle (tel: 32 24 04 43).

FONTAINE-GUÉRARD

east of Rouen
The ruins of this 12th- to 13th-century abbey lie just outside the Forêt de Lyons in beautiful countryside beside the River Andelle.
Open: (guided tours only) Tuesday to Sunday afternoons, April to October.
A popular beauty spot to the southwest near Amfreville is the **Côte des Deux Amants**, a hilltop overlooking the Seine and surrounding countryside.

GAILLARD, CHÂTEAU see ANDELYS, LES

GAILLON

northeast of Evreux
On the south bank of the Seine between Louviers and Vernon, the **castle** here was one of the earliest in France (1502) to show the influence of the Italian Renaissance. Once very grand, and historically important, it now has only an entrance pavilion and one small wing left, though excavations going on may make more of the site eventually.

GISORS

southeast of Rouen
Chiefly notable in this market town on the very eastern edge of Normandy is the **castle**, a key point fortified by both English and French kings during their struggle for Normandy. The first keep was built in the 11th century, and the first curtain walls round the bailey followed under Henry I, around 1125. The present keep was rebuilt by Henry II at the end of the 12th century, and Philip Augustus, having won the castle from King John, built the much higher Tour du Prisonnier (Prisoner's Tower) overlooking the still untrustworthy town. This tower became a prison in the 16th century, when its incarcerated wretches began the drawings and inscriptions still visible inside.
Open: February to November.
Also worth visiting in Gisors is the 13th-century Gothic church of **St-Gervais et St-Protais**.

Tourist Office

3 rue Baléchoux
(tel: 32 27 30 14).

THE SEINE VALLEY

◆◆◆
GIVERNY: MUSÉE
CLAUDE MONET ✓

across the Seine from Vernon
Claude Monet lived at Giverny
from 1883, when he had just
begun to find a market for his
paintings, until his death in 1926,
when he had become a grand
old man of art. Here he laid out
the gardens made famous,
above all, by the *Water Lilies*
series he painted in the first
decade of the new century,
incorporating the distinctive
motif of the arched wooden
bridge that visitors can now
cross during their tour. The
gardens unfortunately went to
ruin, but were left to the country
in 1966 and have recently been
scrupulously restored. Though
well worth a visit, Giverny is
now very popular, and you will
be lucky to miss the crowds.
Perhaps Monet's major
inspiration was the English
garden in Gertrude Jekyll's
style. His borders build up from
small plants at the front to larger
ones at the back, with the very
tallest plants at the centre. One
of his favourite high plants was
lemon yellow mullein, together
with lilies and hollyhocks.
The garden also has a shady
section at the back, by the river
that feeds the lake, with a
bamboo grove and a copse
underplanted with several old
English favourites, such as
Solomon's seal. Some of the
most beautiful planting is
alongside the water, where
some flamboyant autumn golds
and oranges are dramatically

*The bridge and water lilies at
Giverny – Monet's inspiration*

Claude Monet

Born in Paris, in 1840, Claude Monet moved to Le Havre as a child, and it was there that his lifelong connection with Normandy began.

Now familiar to everyone, the term 'Impressionist' was coined by Monet quite by accident. An early exhibition of work by Monet and like-minded artists caused uproar among traditionalist critics, who seized on the title of one of Monet's paintings – *Impression: Sunrise* – as a focus for their mockery of what were seen as slapdash painting techniques.

Monet's revolutionary method as a young man involved painting direct from nature, capturing fleeting effects of light and mood to give the feeling of a particular scene, rather than painstakingly portraying every detail. He had a small boat converted into a studio to enable him to work out of doors on the river; a famous painting by his fellow Impressionist Manet shows him at work in his boat.

In later life Monet worked from his studio at Giverny. Colour, light and mood remained his passionate concerns. He painted several series of pictures of the same subject, for example *Rouen Cathedral* (1892–5), which capture the swim of colour, light and shadow over the stonework. Most famous of his later works – verging on the abstract – is the *Water Lilies* sequence, inspired by his garden.

reflected. In Monet's old studio, now a bookshop, there is every opportunity to study the painter's career – especially in splendid old photographs of the bearded gentleman. In his extreme old age he never left Giverny, but drew all the inspiration for his famous late paintings from the colourful blur in which he now – because of his cataracts – saw his garden. In Monet's lifetime, many young American artists came to study at Giverny. Their works – now famous in their own right – are the basis of the new **Musée Americain Giverny**, close to Monet's house.

Open: both museums Tuesday to Sunday, April to October.

LES ANDELYS see ANDELYS, LES

LOUVIERS
in the Eure Valley, south of Rouen

A rather uneasy combination of half-timbered old town and 20th-century industrial estate, Louviers preserves at its centre a notable Flamboyant Gothic church, **Notre-Dame**. Its wealth of rich decoration was funded by the wool trade – the traditional business of Louviers, now replaced by modern industries. There are several places to stay and to eat in the town, and particularly in the countryside around. Three miles (5km) southeast on the N155 at Vironvay is **Les Saisons** (tel: 32 40 02 56); five miles (8km) north on the N15 at St-Pierre-du-Vauvray is **Hostellerie St-Pierre** (tel: 32 59 93 29).

Tourist Office
10 rue Maréchal Foch (tel: 32 40 04 41).

LYONS-LA-FORÊT
east of Rouen
The beech and oak forest in which the picture-postcard village of Lyons-la-Forêt nestles is one of the finest in Normandy. Wonderful not only for walking and cycling, it has more than its share of tourist sights: apart from **Fontaine-Guérard** (see page 43), the forest includes another abbey ruin, now with a museum of monastic life, at **Mortemer** to the south, where Henry I of England died. You could visit a Romanesque church at **Menesqueville** to the southwest, or a 17th-century château at **Fleury-la-Forêt** to the northeast. The old kitchens here house an exhibition of dolls and toys.

Conveniently situated within reach of all these attractions, and itself offering old buildings to see and antique shops to visit, it is not surprising that the village of Lyons-la-Forêt attracts the crowds in summer.

Accommodation and Restaurants
The old established hostelries of **La Licorne**, place Bensérade (tel: 32 49 62 02) and the **Grand Cerf**, place de la Halle (tel: 32 49 60 44) have no need to cut their prices in order to attract customers. They are restaurants with simple rooms offering good food in typical Normandy surroundings – if you can get in.

Tourist Office
Mairie (tel: 32 49 31 65).

PONT-DE-L'ARCHE
south of Rouen
If you pass this pleasant little village wedged between the Seine and the Forêt de Bord, it is worth stopping to look at its highly ornate Flamboyant Gothic **church**.

ROBERT-LE-DIABLE, CHÂTEAU DE
just southwest of Rouen
This 'castle' is something of a fake: 'Robert the Devil' never was a real person, and the real castle that was once here was largely demolished in the 15th century. Nonetheless, this is a popular place with the residents of nearby Rouen. Visitor attractions among the ruins include displays about the Vikings, William the Conqueror and the former castle. The towers have fine views over the Seine valley, and there is a children's play area.
Open: daily, March to November.

VASCOEUIL, CHÂTEAU DE
east of Rouen
This château on the edge of the Forêt de Lyons is an older red-brick structure modernised in the late 18th century. It became a fashionable country-house *salon* in the mid-19th century and is now a cultural centre holding modern art exhibitions. It also contains a museum concerning the 19th-century French historian Jules Michelet, who did much of his writing here.
Open: daily, afternoons only, March to November.

THE CENTRAL NORTH COAST: CÔTE FLEURIE AND CÔTE DE NACRE

Normandy's best known resorts are those on the so-called **Côte Fleurie** (Flower Coast), between the mouths of the Seine and the Orne. Honfleur, Deauville, Trouville, Cabourg and Houlgate were fashionable when St-Tropez was a fishing village, and are still flourishing. These resorts have a long history and are steeped in nostalgia. Whole families come here, grandparents and grandchildren returning summer after summer to the same chalet or villa or flat. It was on these beaches that the monumental French novelist Marcel Proust remembered watching his beloved Albertine play ball. But the resorts are still going. Their charm is not faded, their paint is not peeling and their appeal to Paris society, as well as to visitors from other places far and near, is undimmed.

The **Côte de Nacre** (Pearl Coast), further west between the rivers Orne and Vire, is a different story, because it was never developed in the same way. It has the same kind of beaches – superb white strands, with dunes rather than the mounds of pebbles of the Pays de Caux – but it has never had the same crowds. Its fame lies rather as the site of the 1944 D-Day landings. These beaches are now commonly known as *Les Plages du Débarquement* (the Landing Beaches), and individually by their wartime code-names – Utah, Omaha, Gold, Juno and Sword. Rusting hulks have been preserved, and museums up and down the coast tell the story again and again in vivid detail. (For the overall story see page 18.)

Smart yachts at berth in the marina on the river Touques at Deauville

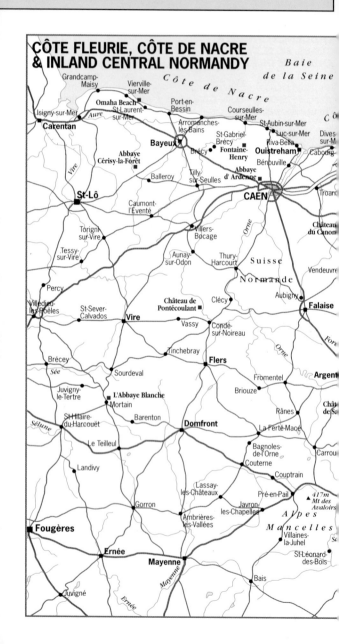

CÔTE FLEURIE, CÔTE DE NACRE & INLAND CENTRAL NORMANDY

Baie de la Seine

Côte de Nacre

Grandcamp-Maisy
Vierville-sur-Mer
Omaha Beach
St-Laurent-sur-Mer
Port-en-Bessin
Courseulles-sur-Mer
Isigny-sur-Mer
Aure
Arromanches-les-Bains
St-Aubin-sur-Mer
Luc-sur-Mer
Côte
Carentan
St-Gabriel-Brécy
Riva-Bella
Dives-sur-M
Bayeux
Fontaine-Henry
Ouistreham
Cabourg
Abbaye Cérisy-la-Forêt
Brécy
Bénouville
Vire
Balleroy
Tilly-sur-Seulles
Abbaye d'Ardenne
St-Lô
CAEN
Troarn
Caumont-l'Éventé
Villers-Bocage
Château du Canon
Torigni-sur-Vire
Orne
Tessy-sur-Vire
Aunay-sur-Odon
Thury-Harcourt
Suisse
Vendeuvre
Percy
Normande
Villedieu-les-Poêles
St-Sever-Calvados
Château de Pontécoulant
Clécy
Aubigny
Falaise
Vire
Vassy
Condé-sur-Noireau
Brécey
Sée
Tinchebray
Orne
Forê
Juvigny-le-Tertre
Sourdeval
Flers
Fromentel
Argent
Briouze
L'Abbaye Blanche
Mortain
St-Hilaire-du-Harcouët
Sélune
Barenton
Domfront
Rânes
Châ de Sa
Le Teilleul
La-Ferté-Macé
Landivy
Bagnoles-de-l'Orne
Couterne
Carrou
Lassay-les-Châteaux
Couptrain
Gorron
Pré-en-Pail
417m Mt des Avaloirs
Ambrières-les-Vallées
Javron-les-Chapelles
Alpes
Fougères
Villaines-la-Juhel
Mancelles
Se
Ernée
St-Léonard-des-Bois
Mayenne
Bais
Juvigné
Ernée
Mayenne

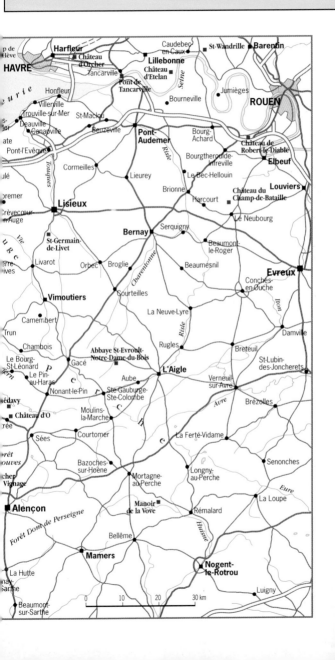

WHAT TO SEE

♦♦♦
ARROMANCHES-LES-BAINS ✓

northeast of Bayeux

This is an unpretentious family holiday resort – with a difference. Visitors flock here because of the extraordinary role Arromanches played in the liberation of France in 1944. Just off the beach can still be seen the remains of one of the two huge artificial ports or 'Mulberry Harbours' which were towed piece by piece from England to help land troops and supplies after the D-Day invasion. The scale of the operation is difficult to comprehend: the ports involved half a million tons of concrete and several miles of floating roads. They worked extremely well.

The large and popular **Musée du Débarquement** (Invasion Museum), on the sea-front, chronicles this remarkable invasion in its collection of photographs, maps, dioramas and military memorabilia.
Open: daily.
Closed: January.

Accommodation

The **Marine**, quai Canada (tel: 31 22 34 19) is a traditional, unspoilt hotel with a good restaurant.

Tourist Office

4 rue Maréchal Joffre (tel: 31 21 47 56).

♦
CABOURG

Cabourg is perhaps the exception to the rule that the Normandy resorts have changed little since their heyday. True, the Grand Hotel – centrepiece of the Edwardian town-plan – still gleams and remains true to the memory of Marcel Proust, who used to stay there. But the main street is gaudy and overpopularised, and you might say Cabourg's finest feature is now the extravagant fake architecture of the mini-golf on the promenade. In summer there are many foreigners, especially British, and few French.

Mulberry Harbour, Arromanches

Cabourg merges into the former inland port of **Dives-sur-Mer**, now a yacht marina. From here Duke William set out to conquer England in ships hardly much bigger than today's yachts. The **Village Guillaume-le-Conquérant** (William the Conqueror's village) is a complex of ancient buildings so much refurbished as to look completely false. Better sights are the church of **Notre-Dame** – particularly the east end, which survives from a fine Romanesque church here – and the 15th-century wooden **market-hall**.

Accommodation and Restaurants

One can eat amid the grand *salons* of the **Pullman Grand Hotel**, promenade Marcel Proust (tel: 31 91 01 79), at reasonable expense considering the hotel's excellent position, right on the beach. It also has some very large bedrooms. There are numerous alternatives in the town, or at the Village Guillaume-le-Conquérant.

Tourist Office

Jardins du Casino (tel: 31 91 01 09).

◆

COURSEULLES-SUR-MER

north of Caen

This is more of a harbour and marina than a beach resort, though it has one. Facing the beach, the **Maison de la Mer** features a 'tunnel' aquarium of local marine life and an extensive sea-shell collection. *Open*: Tuesday to Sunday, April to October.

Accommodation and Restaurants

The **Crémaillère/Le Gytan**, (boulevard de la Plage, tel: 31 37 46 73), is a good hotel. Courseulles is known for its oysters. One can eat them on the quay at the popular **La Pêcherie**, place du 6 Juin (tel: 31 37 45 84).

Tourist Office

54 rue de la Mer (tel: 31 37 46 80)

DEAUVILLE

Deauville is for the rich – and those who like to watch them. Private planes flock to its airport; racehorses are bought and sold here and exclusive shops sell designer labels. In Ciro's café bejewelled, deep-tanned Parisians pay a king's ransom to eat like sparrows. A week's hire of a beach-cabin here might buy you one elsewhere. Not surprisingly, there are few foreigners in this resort. Deauville is for the Parisian jet-set. They take a large flat for the summer in one of the many 'prestige' mansion blocks, or a villa on Mont Canisy behind. In between commuting to Paris, they spend their time yachting, horse-racing, at the casino or at one of the places lining the beach offering *thalassothérapie*. Probably only granny or nanny go to the beach itself with the children. While in Deauville do not miss the ambience of **Les Planches**, a broad avenue of yacht's-deck hardwood extending alongside the beach, till it peters out in down-market neighbouring Bénerville-sur-Mer. Having strolled along Les Planches, looking out over a perfect sandy beach, colourfully tented and meticulously clean, you should then lunch at **Ciro's** café-restaurant to complete the Deauville experience.

Horses, the Planches in summer – there is nothing else to do in Deauville except the film festival, cunningly placed in early September to keep the glamour going just a little longer. The beach-huts bear the names of film stars, and you could say Deauville is a kind of Euro-Hollywood.

Accommodation
Naturally Deauville boasts deluxe hotels such as the **Normandy**, 38 rue Mermoz (tel: 31 98 66 22) or the **Royal**, boulevard E Cornuché (tel: 31 98 66 33). More modest ones exist, but Deauville is not that kind of place.

Restaurants
Except for **Le Spinnaker**, 52 rue Mirabeau (tel: 31 88 24 40), which is very good and not extravagantly expensive, and **Ciro's**, promenade des Planches (tel: 31 88 18 10) for lunch, it is difficult to find anything beyond an overpriced *croque monsieur* in Deauville. Try Trouville.

Tourist Office
place de la Mairie (tel: 31 88 21 43).

DIVES-SUR-MER see CABOURG

GRANDCAMP-MAISY
northeast of Carentan
Grandcamp is a fishing port and marina frequented mainly by seafarers and those addicted to the shellfish abundant on its

rocks. The atmosphere is different from the usual run of holiday places, and there are good fish restaurants. Two modest places are **La Marée**, quai Cheron (tel: 31 22 60 55), or the hotel **Duguesclin**, 4 quai Crampon (tel: 31 22 64 22).

HONFLEUR ✓

Stone and timber-framed houses, winding streets and open quays, ships and easels, an old-world ambience and a thriving, humming atmosphere – Honfleur is picturesque in the good old sense, a postcard of a town but a living one. Even though it gets very full in summer, it never loses its spirit or its character. A series of galleries and artists' shops line the **Vieux Bassin** (Old Harbour), which was the new harbour when it was dug out in the 17th century, but was itself replaced by the other harbour basins in the 19th. Honfleur's artistic tradition goes back to the generation before the Impressionists – to Gustave Courbet and Eugène Boudin, who was born here. The **Musée Boudin** houses a representative selection of his and other 19th-century painting.
Open: Wednesday to Monday. *Closed*: weekday mornings in winter, and the first half of February.

Other museums are the **Musée du Vieux Honfleur**, full of bygone bourgeois and folk artefacts, and the **Musée de la Marine** (Maritime Museum).
Open: both museums daily in summer; Saturday afternoon and Sunday, February to mid-June.

Just back from the port, the
remarkable 15th-century
wooden church of **Ste-
Catherine**, overlooking the
market place, was built by
Honfleur's skilled shipwrights in
thanksgiving that the English
had finally departed. During the
following years Honfleur
rivalled Rouen and Dieppe in its
seafaring enterprise, and
Samuel de Champlain founded
Québec after sailing from
Honfleur in 1608.
The greatest pleasure of
Honfleur is to wander its streets,
quays and squares, threading
your way through alleys made
narrow by tall, overhanging
timber-framed houses. Take
time to potter or to buy, to eat or
drink, and above all to soak up
the atmosphere.

Accommodation
Honfleur's most famous hotel is
La Ferme St-Siméon, rue Marais
(outside town towards Trouville,
tel: 31 89 23 61). Once a fuelling
stop for poor Impressionists, it is
still thoroughly Norman, and

beautifully run, with a fine
restaurant – though prices have
kept up with the times.
Generally, Honfleur's hotels are
noticeably expensive, but
several are well recommended.
These include the **Hostellerie du
Belvédère** (a good restaurant-
with-rooms), 36 rue Emile-
Rénouf (tel: 31 89 08 13); **Le
Castel Albertine**, 19 cours
Manuel (tel: 31 98 85 56); and **Le
Cheval Blanc**, 2 quai des
Passagers (tel: 31 81 65 00).

Restaurants
There is no shortage. **Au P'tit
Marayeur**, 4 rue Haute (tel: 31
98 84 23), is in one of Honfleur's
many pretty streets. Together
with the **Belvédère** (see
Accommodation, above) it is
perhaps best for value.
L'Assiette Gourmande, 8 place
Ste-Cathérine (tel: 31 89 24 88),
is another in the tourist area,
but still excellent. Other reliable
restaurants include the nearby

*Honfleur harbour – one of the
classic sights of Normandy*

La Lieutenance, 12 place Ste-Catherine (tel: 31 89 07 52), and **L'Ancrage**, 12 rue Montpensier (tel: 31 89 00 70). The décor is sometimes in modern style, but most of the houses are timbered inside as well as out. In spite of the many restaurants, few are empty during the season, and the place fairly pulsates with family *bonhomie* at the cheek-by-jowl tables. So start looking early if you haven't booked. Some restaurants may seem a little expensive for what they are, but the food is more than adequate – especially fish, of course, but succulent steaks as well.

Tourist Office
place Boudin (tel: 31 89 23 30).

Eugene Boudin
A generation ahead of the Impressionists, Boudin was a native of Honfleur and many of his works are local scenes. Art historians have tended to pigeon-hole Boudin as the precursor of Impressionism and move on, paying little attention to his pictures themselves – a pity, because the paintings repay closer study. Boudin specialised in small, horizontal pictures of beach parties, often seen from a distance with wide skies behind, and with light and shade featuring prominently. He befriended the young Monet – 16 years his junior – who did not, at that time, like Boudin's work. Nevertheless, Boudin was one of the exhibitors at what later became known as the First Impressionist Exhibition, in 1874.

HOULGATE
Situated between Deauville and Cabourg, Houlgate is a good choice, avoiding the excesses of either. This old-fashioned family resort, with turn-of-the-century villas and few modern buildings, has fine, long, flat sandy beaches but also rocks suitable for curious children. High cliffs to the east include the **Falaise des Vaches Noires** (Black Cow Cliff). The name was coined to describe the broken rocks covered by seaweed at its base.

Hotel and Restaurant
Le 1900, 17 rue Bains (tel: 31 28 77 77) is a central, simple restaurant-with-rooms.

Tourist Office
boulevard des Belges (tel: 31 24 34 79).

LUC-SUR-MER
north of Caen
A continuation of the resorts of Lion-sur-Mer and Riva-Bella, Luc-sur-Mer has an excellent **beach** and **gardens**, and deserves a mention, as does a local hotel called **Beau Rivage**, 1 rue Charcot (tel: 31 96 49 51).

Tourist Office
rue Charcot (tel: 31 97 33 25).

OUISTREHAM
north of Caen
This port and marina at the mouth of the River Orne is the dock for ferries from Portsmouth (Brittany Ferries). Places of interest here include a **lighthouse**, a small **Musée du Débarquement** (Invasion

Museum) and a Romanesque **church**. Ouistreham is full of small villas – a suburb of a resort. It runs into **Riva-Bella**, wtih its long, sandy **beach**.

Hotel and Restaurant
A recommended hotel and restaurant is the **Broche d'Argent**, place Général de Gaulle (tel: 31 97 12 16).

Tourist Office
place Thomas (tel: 31 97 18 63).

◆
PORT-EN-BESSIN
northwest of Bayeux
This small working fishing port is claustrophobically flanked by cliffs and has no beach – rather unexpected on this coast. There is a museum of shipwrecks from the D-Day landings.
Open: daily, June to September, also Easter and Pentecost.

Restaurant
One good fish restaurant is **La Foncée**, 12 rue Letourneur (tel: 31 21 71 66).

◆◆
TROUVILLE
Trouville is a less expensive, smaller version of Deauville, on the other side of the River Touques. It has a similar but shorter **boardwalk** and a similar but less smart **children's train** regularly touring the streets. Trouville is more of a family place than Deauville, and more genteel. It also has better architecture, better restaurants, and (on the port) a **fish market** that is unbeatable.

Accommodation
There are several very pleasant small family hotels in Trouville near the beach and in the heart

Shellfish at Trouville's fish market comes in all shapes – and sizes

of the town but they are all booked up by August. Try the quiet **Carmen**, 24 rue Carnot (tel: 31 88 35 43); or the small but luxurious **St James**, 16 rue de la Plage (tel: 31 88 05 23). More anonymous modern ones are the **Beach**, 1 quai Albert (tel: 31 98 12 00), and the **Mercure**, place Maréchal Foch (tel: 31 87 38 38).

Restaurants
The famous restaurant is **Les Vapeurs**, 160 boulevard Moureaux (tel: 31 88 15 24), but **Le Central** next door (tel: 31 88 13 68) is less brassy and perhaps even better. Boulevard Fernand Moureaux is packed with restaurants, and there are quite a number of adequate, reasonable places to eat.

Tourist Office
32–36 boulevard Moureaux (tel: 31 88 36 19).

CAEN

Like Rouen and Le Havre, Caen
suffered terribly in World War
II. But though there are clear
signs of destruction, it has kept
its old-world charm. That is due
to its site, which has both level
areas and hills, and to the easy
pace of its streets and squares –
it is more open than Rouen –
and to the beauty of its stone,
the yellow-grey, fine-grained
Caen stone which was also
shipped by the Normans to
England for use in building. In
this century its ore deposits
made Caen a steel town, and it
is surrounded by industry, but
its population is only a third of
Rouen's. The port of Caen is at
Ouistreham (see page 54).
Caen was the creation of
William the Conqueror, and its
centre is bounded by his three
great works, the Abbaye aux
Hommes to the west, the
Abbaye aux Dames to the east,
and the castle overlooking the
city in between. 'Guillaume le
Conquérant' is a recurrent
theme in Caen.
Open spaces in the town
include the former **Cimetière
St-Nicolas** (cemetery of St
Nicholas), which has a
Romanesque gate, and the
Jardin des Plantes (Botanical
Gardens).
Just outside the town to the
west, off the D9 to St-Lô, the
Abbaye d'Ardenne is a fine
ruined 13th-century abbey.
There is access from the
expressway round Caen to the
Mémoriale pour la Paix on its
northwestern side. Opened in
1988, the centrepiece of the
memorial is a museum of World

War II, presented as a
monument to future peace.
Audio-visual presentations trace
the events that led up to the war
and portray life in occupied
France, ending with a message
of peace and hope for the future.
The memorial centre is a
convenient stopping-place, with
a restaurant and bank.
Open: daily, except Christmas
Day and first half of January.

WHAT TO SEE

ABBAYE AUX DAMES

William the Conqueror is said to
have founded Caen's two
abbeys, one for men and one for
women, in return for papal
dispensation to marry his cousin
Matilda. However, such
dispensations were never a
problem and the real point was
to create burial churches or

mausoleums, one for himself and one for Matilda.

Matilda's foundation – the Abbaye aux Dames – is not so large, glorious or well furnished (or as well visited) as the Abbaye aux Hommes. The nave of its church – La Trinité – belongs to a slightly later, more ornate style of Romanesque, though it was actually founded earlier – in 1062. Matilda's plain tomb is in the chancel, which has been altered, though it still has its massive 11th-century barrel-vault. There are several figurative capitals in the church and in the crypt, including one with an elephant.

Open: daily; guided tours at 14.30 and 16.00hrs.

The Abbaye aux Hommes. The church of St-Etienne is flanked by 18th-century monastic buildings

◆◆◆
ABBAYE AUX HOMMES ✓

Begun in 1066, the Abbaye aux Hommes has one of the grandest Norman Romanesque churches, St-Etienne. It is of enormous length and height for its day. It has wide, spacious galleries and a tall central crossing-tower (rebuilt) of the kind English cathedrals, such as Ely and Norwich, copied. Originally the nave had a wooden roof, but this was replaced in the early 12th century by a stone vault which was an important precursor of Gothic style. The east end, not completed until the 13th century, has a normal early Gothic vault. The outside view of the west end of the church is unique: a fortress of a church, built like a Norman keep.

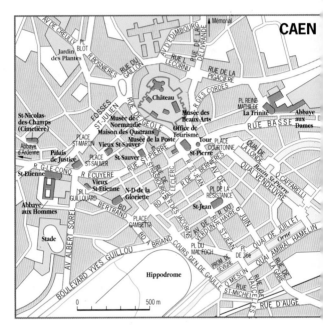

Usually Gothic rose windows were inserted later, but this front has kept its primitive aspect. It recalls the great Carolingian churches, but has greater height – looking forward to Gothic.

The obvious thing missing from William's last resting place is his tomb – unfortunately destroyed in the 16th century. Some handsome church furniture of later date and the 18th-century monastic buildings (now the *Mairie* or town hall) are also worth seeing.

Open: guided tours daily.

◆◆
CASTLE

William's castle at Caen does not seem to have been very imposing. But later both English and French kings strengthened and refortified the site in their struggle for Normandy. By the 17th century, it had become obsolete both militarily and strategically, so was left derelict. Buildings grew up in its extensive bailey. The destruction wrought during World War II reduced it to a pristine archaeological site, in which the ruins are laid bare and two modern museums now stand.

You enter the castle through one of two barbicans added in the 13th century and improved in the 14th and 15th. They once guarded drawbridges over a moat. Inside you can see the remains of the original keep, built in stone in the early 12th century by Henry I of England,

nd the so-called *Echiquier* (Exchequer), a palace of the same date, also the Chapelle St-Georges (St George's Chapel). The curtain walls are due to the French king, Philip Augustus. The larger of the two museums in the bailey, the **Musée des Beaux-Arts**, has paintings from the Renaissance period, a substantial collection of baroque pictures by leading French and Dutch names, some good 18th-century French work and a collection featuring virtually all the best known French artists of the 19th century, from Romantics to Impressionists. The smaller **Musée de Normandie** is a historical museum concentrating on Norman rural life, with some excellent models and artefacts. There is also a good archaeological section.
Open: castle, free access; Musée de Normandie, Wednesday to Monday. *Closed*: some holidays.

◆

MUSÉE DE LA POSTE ET DES TECHNIQUES DE COMMUNICATION
rue St-Pierre
This museum of post and telecommunications is some-thing out of the ordinary, and will particularly interest children. French telecommunications are some of the most advanced in Europe, so adults can catch up, too. Besides the sophisticated systems of today, the museum also displays old equipment.
Open: Tuesday to Saturday, April to December. *Closed*: mornings, except in summer.

Accommodation
There is no very special hotel in Caen, but two with good food, both near the castle, are **Le Dauphin**, 29 rue Gémare (tel: 31 86 22 26) and the **Relais des Gourmets**, 15 rue de Geôle (tel: 31 86 06 01).

Restaurants
The outstanding restaurant is **La Bourride**, 15 rue Vaugueux (tel: 31 93 50 76) – unassailably the best in town, some say in Normandy. It has a very Norman setting and equally Norman specialities, in both fish and meat. Nor is it the only one: **L'Ecaille**, 13 rue de Geôle (tel: 31 86 06 01), has outstanding fish and shellfish, or alternatively, try the usually crowded **Le Boeuf Ferré**, 10 rue Froide (located off rue Croisiers, tel: 31 85 36 40), or **Alcide**, 1 place Courtonne (tel: 31 44 18 06).

Tourist Office
1 place St-Pierre (tel: 31 27 14 14).

◆

ST-PIERRE
below the castle, in the centre of town (on rue St-Pierre)
This mostly 14th-century church has some splendid carving and an extraordinarily ornate early 16th-century east end, neither quite late Gothic nor early Renaissance. Opposite is the **Hôtel d'Escoville**, a merchant's mansion of the 1530s. Nearby streets feature half-timbered houses of equal antiquity. Few such buildings have survived in Caen, and almost all suffered heavy damage by bombs and fire in 1944.

BAYEUX

For visitors (and there are
many of them, especially in
summer), Bayeux is centred on
the museum housing the
famous Bayeux tapestry. There
is more to the well-preserved
medieval town than this,
however. Unlike many towns
and villages in Normandy,
Bayeux escaped damage in
World War II, and it has kept its
historic feel. Do not miss its fine
cathedral, its compact web of
interesting old streets, such as
the rue St-Malo and the rue St-
Jean, and the fine half-timbered
post inn, the **Lion d'Or**, which
still serves excellent food.

WHAT TO SEE

BAYEUX TAPESTRY see
CENTRE GUILLAUME LE
CONQUÉRANT

◆◆
CATHEDRAL

The west end and the crypt
date from the time of Odo,
Bishop of Bayeux, one of
William the Conqueror's close
followers. His cathedral was
completed in 1077, but much of
this original church was
subsequently rebuilt. The
massive cross-ribs in the left
tower are very early work, but
most of the rest of the cathedral
is 12th- and 13th-century.
Its splendid nave and choir, lit
by a full set of enormous
stained-glass windows, are
beautiful High Gothic work.
The nave is rather narrow
because, despite the new
Gothic elevations, the church
was built on an original
Romanesque plan.

◆◆◆
CENTRE GUILLAUME
LE CONQUÉRANT ✓

rue de Nesmond
This is the new museum
housing the **Bayeux tapestry**
(*Tapisserie de la Reine
Mathilde*). In the old days you
might have taken your time to
look at this extraordinary 11th-
century embroidery with the
story of the Conquest of
England – but not any more.
Before reaching the tapestry,
visitors are led through a series
of displays explaining the
background to the events it
depicts. Much of this is useful,
but if the museum is crowded
(as it usually is in summer), you
have shuffled in a queue for too
long by the time you reach the
tapestry and your children may
be tired. The fact remains that,
you are in Normandy, the
Bayeaux tapestry has to be
seen. The 230-foot (70-m)
embroidery is a crucial
document, not just for the
historical events of the
Conquest, but for many
different dimensions of Norman
life – what the castles looked
like before stone replaced the
original wood; how oaths were
sworn and treaties made; how
people saddled and rode their
horses. It is well known that the
'tapestry' is really an
embroidery, but not that the
end of it has been lost, so it
breaks off well before William's
coronation. It used to hang in
the cathedral, and was
probably made for Odo, Bishop
of Bayeux, in an English
workshop, perhaps in
Canterbury. The tale of the

dispute for the crown of England is told from the Norman angle, putting the Saxon Harold in the wrong, but it is worth remembering that William had had the support of the previous Saxon king, Edward the Confessor, who admired Norman culture and had introduced it to England well before the Conquest. How much of a 'conquest' the Norman takeover really was is still controversial among historians.
Open: daily, all year.

◆

MUSÉE BARON-GÉRARD
north of the cathedral
A small permanent collection of paintings is displayed here in an old house of some charm. Some of Baron Gérard's own pictures are included in the collection: he was a rather theatrical follower of the great neoclassicist J L David in the early 19th century. The museum also represents the decorative arts with its displays of porcelain, ceramics and lace.
Open: daily, all year.

◆

MUSÉE MEMORIAL DE LA BATAILLE DE NORMANDIE
boulevard F Ware
The Battle of Normandy Museum is in Bayeux because Bayeux was the first city liberated by the advancing Allied forces in 1944. It is an audio-visual paradise of models and dioramas, together with original military equipment, sound effects, and film footage from the campaign.
Open: daily, all year.

The cathedral, seen from the east

Accommodation
The **Lion d'Or**, 71 rue St-Jean (tel: 31 92 06 90) is a traditional inn with a popular restaurant. There are other good hotels in the city, but none delivers quite the same experience. At the other end of the scale, the Youth Hostel **Les Sablons**, rondpoint de Vaucelles (tel: 31 92 15 22), is not too far outside the centre.

Restaurants
Apart from the **Lion d'Or**, above, there is no obvious choice, but try **La Rapière**, 53 rue St-Jean (tel: 31 92 94 79).

Tourist Office
1 rue des Cuisiniers (tel: 31 92 16 26).

INLAND CENTRAL NORMANDY: AUGE, PERCHE AND SUISSE NORMANDE

If Normandy has a centre it is the **Pays d'Auge**, the region centred on Lisieux, traversed by the rivers Dives, Touques and Risle and spread across the *départements* of Calvados, Eure and Orne. This is archetypal Normandy, a green land of orchards and meadows grazed by spotted cows, and peppered with traditional *chaumières* – thatched and timber-framed houses or barns. From the orchards come the apples to make cider and Calvados, and from the cows the milk to make Camembert, invented near Vimoutiers in the Auge. The countryside is lush and varied, undulating and well covered with trees.

South of the Auge, in the region called the **Perche**, the houses revert to stone. There is a good scattering of turrets – perhaps the influence of the neighbouring Loire. The country is similar to the Auge, but the Perche has been known more for its horses than for its cows (there is a Percheron breed), and more for its *boudin* (black pudding) than for its cheese. There are some dense forests, too, and it is excellent territory for ramblers (*randonneurs*).

Due south of Caen, the **Suisse Normande** ('Norman Switzerland') is so called not because it has any real mountains but because it is the kind of place to go camping, walking or canoeing. Through the middle of this country of wooded hills, the River Orne

Normandy's countryside at its peaceful best – farmland in the Auge

courses through a series of rocky gorges.

One more region that could be mentioned is the **Ouche**, between the River Eure to the east and the Auge and Perche to the west. But with all these regions, borders are vague and still leave great tracts of land without a convenient label. There is no dramatic change in the countryside as you travel through central Normandy, although it becomes a little drier towards the west. It is all quite lush enough, however, to make a superb touring or rambling holiday, or a delightful backdrop to a more indulgent eating-and-drinking stopover, staying either in one of the many delightful half-timbered inns or in one of the superb châteaux-hotels.

Dedicated sightseers will find plenty of notable châteaux, churches and abbeys in central Normandy, many of which are mentioned in **What to See**, below. However, a whistle-stop tour of the 'sights' would miss the point. Essentially this is a region for leisurely, and perhaps unplanned, touring. Almost wherever you go, you will be sure to discover unpretentious, timeless villages, bustling old country towns full of atmosphere, rural lanes and by-ways well off the beaten track, and a countryside that has for the most part escaped the ravages of late 20th-century agriculture and development. Abandon your schedules, arm yourself with a good map and – most of all – take your time!

Alençon's lace museum

WHAT TO SEE
(See map on pages 48–9)

ALENÇON
This delightful old Norman town lies close to the centre of a huge conservation area – the **Parc Naturel Régional Normandie-Maine**. Alençon has its own forests – **Perseigne** to the east, **Ecouves** to the north – and, to the west, the hills called the **Alpes Mancelles**. Both Perseigne and Ecouves are mixed forests; in the Forêt d'Ecouves boar are reputed still to roam.

Alençon itself – famed in the past for its lace-making – has a church and a museum worth visiting. **Notre-Dame** is a Flamboyant Gothic church with fine stonework and stained glass; it also has a chapel commemorating Ste-Thérèse of

Lisieux, who was baptised here. The **Musée des Beaux-Arts et de la Dentelle** (Museum of Fine Art and Lace) contains two disparate collections, one of paintings and one of lace. Its lace industry was implanted in Alençon by Louis XIV's minister Colbert – a kind of parallel to the royal workshops that made Gobelins famous for tapestries, or Sèvres for porcelain. Certainly the finest lacework in France was made here. The museum also has a collection of lace made by its European rivals, especially Venice. *Open*: Tuesday to Sunday.

Accommodation and Restaurants

The best hotel (and quite reasonable) must be the **Chapeau Rouge**, 1 boulevard Duchamp (tel: 33 26 20 23). It has no restaurant, so you will have to go out – perhaps to the edge of town, to **Au Petit Vatel**, 72 place Desmeulles (tel: 33 26 23 78).

Tourist Office

Maison d'Ozé, 1 place Lamagdelaine (tel: 33 26 11 36).

◆

ARGENTAN

A historic small town with two Flamboyant Gothic churches, several hotels and restaurants and a good market, Argentan is bordered by the Suisse Normande to the west and the Forêt de Gouffern to the east. This makes it a good touring centre, with plenty of places of interest within easy reach. Famous for its lace – '*le point d'Argentan*' – the town was also a key position in the fighting that followed D-Day in 1944. Like so many other Norman towns, it suffered heavy damage.

Tourist Office

1 place du Marché (tel: 33 67 12 48).

AUBIGNY see FALAISE

Lace-making in Normandy

Lace as we know it was probably first produced in Flanders, but by the 17th century the lace of Venice was considered the finest. By then, lace was an essential part of fashionable costume. Schools of lace-making sprang up elsewhere in Europe, including those at Alençon, Bayeux and Argentan in Normandy. Each lace-making centre developed its own stitches and techniques, and both needlepoint and bobbin lace were found.

Many hours of painstaking, detailed work went into this hand-made lace, and patterns were a jealously guarded 'trade secret'.

The 19th century saw the burgeoning of the machine lace industry, notably at Nottingham in England. Passable lace could be made in a fraction of the time taken to produce the hand-made article, and commercial lace-making by hand began to die out.

Normandy produces little hand-made lace today, but examples of the exquisite workmanship of the past can be seen in the museums at Alençon and Bayeux.

The lake and casino at Bagnoles

◆
BAGNOLES-DE-L'ORNE
Bagnoles is a spa town, and though it is unique in Normandy it has the neat and tidy air of spas everywhere. The municipal gardens and casino by the lake are classic spa-town architecture. However, Bagnoles today is also a centre for rambling or cycling in the nearby **Forêt d'Ecouves** (see page 63).

Accommodation and Restaurants
Bagnoles has several well-run hotels; one especially worth noting for its food is the **Manoir du Lys**, out on the D235 towards Juvigny (tel: 33 37 80 69). This comfortable hotel is a converted 19th-century hunting lodge in spacious grounds.

Tourist Office
place de la République (tel: 33 37 85 66).

◆◆
BALLEROY, CHÂTEAU DE
southwest of Bayeux
Here is a remarkable and well-preserved house in the French classical style. Under the royal architect François Mansart, it rose in one build from 1626 to 1636, and has kept its interior decoration, by Charles de la Fosse, largely unaltered. Externally, though severe, the house is a fitting and rather splendid climax to a sequence of gatehouse, drive, service quarters and formal gardens designed by the famous French landscaper Le Nôtre. A **balloon museum** has been set up in recent years.
Open: Thursday to Tuesday, mid-April to October.

◆◆
BEAUMESNIL, CHÂTEAU DE
between Bernay and Conches
This château is almost exactly contemporary (1633–40) with Balleroy (see page 65) and very similar in design, though the façade is considerably more enriched. It, too, has beautiful gardens, including a lake, and an additional museum, this one of book-binding.
Open: Friday to Monday afternoons, mid-May to mid-September.

◆
BEC-HELLOUIN, LE
southeast of Pont-Audemer
The fame of the historic **abbey** here on the River Risle goes back to the 11th century. In 1034 Herluin renounced the world and founded his own small hermitage here. It grew, beyond his original intentions, into a leading religious and intellectual centre. From it sprang the first two Norman archbishops of Canterbury, Lanfranc and St Anselm – the most distinguished theologian of his time.
The monastery remained in being until the Revolution, when, like many others in Normandy, it was pulled apart for the stone; monks returned in 1948 and built a new church beside the ruins. Today there is a rather incongruous **car museum** nearby.
Open: Wednesday to Monday.

Accommodation
The **Auberge de l'Abbaye** (tel: 32 44 86 02) offers simple bedrooms and good Norman cooking in a delightful village house.

◆
BELLÊME
Overlooking a superb oak forest in the Perche region, Bellême is an attractive, well-preserved little town on a hill. Little remains of its 15th-century ramparts, but there are some interesting old houses and a couple of hotels and restaurants. A pleasant short walk in the nearby **Forêt de Bellême** is round the lake known as **l'Etang de la Herse**.

Tourist Office
Hôtel de Ville (tel: 33 73 09 69).

◆
BERNAY
This historic Norman town grew up around the now ruined abbey church in its centre. Founded in 1013 by William the Conqueror's grandmother, this was later rebuilt, but some very early parts remain. Close by is a small **museum** of local crafts.
Open: Wednesday to Monday. The church of **Ste-Croix** dates from the 14th and 15th centuries. Among Bernay's half-timbered houses are some typically Norman hotels and restaurants. There is also a pleasant walk along the **Promenade des Monts**.

Tourist Office
29 rue Thiers (tel: 32 43 32 08).

◆
BOURG-ST-LÉONARD, LE
The late 18th-century **château** here has fine contemporary interiors including tapestries and Louis XV furniture.
Open: Thursday to Tuesday, mid-June to mid-September.
Closed: mornings, except first half of August.

BRÉCY
east of Bayeux
Brécy has a 13th-century parish church and, round the small 17th-century **château**, some very pretty formal gardens.
Open: daily, April to October.

BRIONNE
northeast of Bernay
Another charming market town, Brionne has an 11th-century *donjon* (keep), a 15th-century church with a fine wooden roof, and a craft museum, the **Maison de Normandie**.
Open: all year.
Closed: Wednesday, October to May.
There are two excellent hotel-restaurants, **Auberge Vieux Donjon**, 19 rue Soie (tel: 32 44 80 62), and **Logis de Brionne**, 1 place St-Denis (tel: 32 44 81 73).

Le Bec-Hellouin village

Tourist Office
place de l'Eglise (tel: 32 45 70 51).

CANAPVILLE
southeast of Deauville
The 15th-century timbered manor here is worth visiting as a fine example of traditional Norman building style.
Open: Wednesday to Monday afternoons, mid-June to August; weekends and holidays only out of season.

CANON, CHÂTEAU DE
southeast of Caen
This minor château is important for its 18th-century gardens. Embellished by statues and follies, the gardens are formal but influenced by contemporary English landscaping.
Open: Wednesday to Monday afternoons, July to September; weekend and holiday afternoons, Easter to June.

The Pont du Vey at Clécy

◆

CARROUGES

east of Bagnoles-de-l'Orne
Domain for centuries of the
prominent Le Veneur de
Thillières family, the **château** just
outside this hilltop village is a
rambling but impressive mixture
of ages and styles with a
splendid early Renaissance
gatehouse and surrounded by a
moat. Its interiors also date from
several periods.
Open: Wednesday to Monday.
Closed: some holidays.

◆

CERISY-LA-FORÊT

between St-Lô and Bayeux
The shorn abbey here is a
Romanesque gem in a now
greatly reduced beech forest.
The church has lost four of its
former seven bays, but remains
worth seeing.

◆

CHAMBOIS

northeast of Argentan
The ruined keep at Chambois,
built under Henry II of England

though since modified, was
long a key strongpoint of the
region. The village's later fame
is remembered in a monument
in the square which
commemorates its key role at
the end of the Battle of
Normandy in 1944.

◆

CHAMP-DE-BATAILLE

southwest of Rouen
Champ-de-Bataille is one of
Normandy's grandest châteaux.
The late 17th-century building
has predominantly 18th-century
neoclassical interiors. It is now
also a country club with a golf-
course.
Open: afternoons, April to
October.

◆◆

CLÉCY

A good centre for exploring the
Suisse Normande, Clécy is an
attractive village on the River
Orne. Several walks are
signposted; one goes to the
**Musée du Chemin de Fer
Miniature** (model railway
museum).
Open: daily; mornings only
October to Easter.
There is also a craft museum at
the **Manoir de Placy.**
Open: guided tours daily
afternoons only, July and August.
Cafés and restaurants cluster
round the **Pont du Vey**, and
landmarks and viewpoints
further afield within walking
distance include the **Viaduc de
la Lande** and the **Pain de
Sucre**. Paintings of the Suisse
Normande by the artist André
Hardy can be seen in the
Musée Hardy.
Open: daily, Easter to
September.

Accommodation and Restaurants

Several good hotel-restaurants include **Le Moulin du Vey**, by the Vey bridge (tel: 31 69 71 08).

Tourist Office

Mairie, place de l'Eglise (tel: 31 69 79 95).

◆

CONCHES-EN-OUCHE

Conches is another small Norman town with all the traditional ingredients: a large forest nearby; a ruined castle; a charming 16th-century church with notable stained glass; good restaurants including **La Coque Blanche**, 18 place Carnot (tel: 32 30 01 54).

Tourist Office

Maison des Arts, place Aristide-Briand (tel: 32 30 91 82).

◆

CRÉVECOEUR-EN-AUGE

west of Lisieux

The village called 'Heartbreak in the Auge' has a charming ruined **castle** with 500-year-old farm buildings in the bailey, restored and converted into a small museum of oil prospecting. Art exhibitions are also held here.
Open: afternoons, mid-February to mid-November.

◆

DOMFRONT

The castle here was once very grand and as late as 1578 withstood siege when held by the extraordinary character Gabriel de Montgomery, who killed the French king Henri II in a tournament, and was later

beheaded. Beside the castle ruins and a Romanesque church there is a rather self-conscious old town, empty of hotels and restaurants, which are to be found in the new town at the bottom of the hill.
Two modest hotels, both with restaurants, are the **Poste**, rue Maréchal Foch (tel: 33 38 51 00), and the **France**, rue Mont-St-Michel (tel: 33 38 51 44).

Tourist Office

rue Dr Barrabé (tel: 33 38 53 97).

◆◆

FALAISE

The birthplace of William the Conqueror in 1027, Falaise has a fine **castle** – much bigger than the one he occupied, but on the same site. The town's name (French for 'cliff') comes from the castle's site – a great bluff rearing over the valley. The keep, with outjutting chapel, is 12th-century, built by Henry I; the cylindrical Tour de Talbot was added in the early 13th century, and the curtain walls slightly later.
Open: daily, except Monday and Tuesday in winter.
The rest of the town, which suffered badly in World War II, is somewhat characterless, but has adequate hotels and good-value restaurants. There is not a wide choice: for hotels try the **Normandie**, 4 rue Amiral Courbet (tel: 31 90 18 26) or the **Poste**, 38 rue Clémenceau (tel: 31 90 13 14). A nearby restaurant is **La Fine Fourchette**, 52 rue Clémenceau (tel: 31 90 08 59). The tiny village of **Aubigny**, just north of Falaise, is worth visiting

for the outstanding tombs in its church. They show six former lords of the manor, all dressed up in a row ready for the Almighty.

Tourist Office
32 rue Clemenceau (tel: 31 90 17 26).

FONTAINE-HENRY
northwest of Caen
The grand **château** here was constructed slowly from the end of the 15th century through the 16th, and fascinatingly evolves – from south to north – from Gothic into classical. Inside there is a notable collection mostly of French paintings.
Open: Wednesday to Monday, mid-June to mid-September; weekend and holiday afternoons Easter to mid-June and mid-September to October.

HARAS DU PIN see PIN, LE

HARCOURT
southeast of Brionne
The **château** at Harcourt fronts a lovely ruined bailey in the unusual and tranquil setting of a mature arboretum. This is the ancestral home of the Harcourt family, whose name crops up again and again in French history. Members of the family have been involved in military and political affairs from the 11th century to the present day. Their castle here has suffered various damage, by warfare and by fire, over the centuries, but remains surprisingly well preserved.
Open: afternoons, mid-March to mid-November.

LE PIN see PIN, LE

LISIEUX
Lisieux is an historic bishopric and is today the leading town of the Auge region. It is also the home town of Ste-Thérèse of Lisieux, which has transformed it into a lesser Lourdes. The pilgrim traffic to her house (**'Les Buissonets'**) and to the **Basilique Ste-Thérèse** – an enormous sugar-cake of a church, consecrated in the 1950s – is considerable. Lisieux has a charming 13th-century **cathedral**, with a renowned Flamboyant Gothic chapel built by one of its bishops in the mid-15th century. While in Lisieux, take few minutes to wander among the timbered-framed buildings of its old streets, and to visit the market – good for all sorts of traditional Normandy fare.

Tourist Office
11 rue d'Alençon (tel: 31 62 08 41

LONGNY-AU-PERCHE
east of Mortagne-au-Perche
Though it is a pleasant little town well situated for exploring the wooded countryside of the eastern Perche, Longny has only a few hotels and restaurants. The chapel of Notre-Dame-de-Pitié dates from the 16th century.

Tourist Office
Hôtel de Ville (tel: 33 73 66 23)

MORTAGNE-AU-PERCHE
This attractive and unspoilt hill town is a good base for a stay the Perche countryside. The

The Percheron – Normandy's Own Horse

The Perche region of Normandy, with Mortagne as its traditional capital, has long been famous for breeding horses. The best known, taking its name from the district, is the Percheron, a heavily built grey or black breed which was first reared by a small group of farmers in the Perche during the early 19th century – though the horse's ancestry is said to be traceable as far back as the Crusades.

Energetic yet sure-footed, tremendously strong yet docile and easily broken, Percherons were highly prized for farm work in the days before tractors. Today, they may be less sought after for agricultural purposes in many countries, but Percherons have been bred all over the world and their fine qualities are still much valued in cross-breeding.

MORTAIN

The historic town of Mortain has an attractive setting by river and forest. The 13th-century church of **St-Evroult** survived substantial war damage to Mortain in 1944. Nearby is the **Abbaye Blanche**, a 12th-century Cistercian church whose plainness reflects the early asceticism of the order. *Open*: Wednesday to Monday. *Closed*: Sunday morning. There is good rambling countryside to the north of Mortain, around the valley of the River Sée. Nearer at hand, a steep track just off the Avenue de l'Abbaye-Blanche leads to the **Grande Cascade**, an 80-foot (25-m) waterfall. Reasonable accommodation and meals are available in the town. Two modest hotels serving local fare are the **Poste**, 1 place des Arcades (tel: 33 59 00 05), and the **Cheval Blanc**, (tel: 33 59 00 60).

Tourist Office

place Hôtel de Ville (tel: 33 59 19 74).

church of **Notre-Dame** is a blend of Flamboyant Gothic and Renaissance styles, with some fine 18th-century carvings.

Restaurants

Two excellent, traditional restaurants are the **Genty-Home**, 4 rue Notre-Dame (tel: 33 25 11 53), and the **Tribunal**, 4 place du Palais (tel: 33 25 04 77). Both of these have rooms available.

Tourist Office

place Général de Gaulle (tel: 33 85 11 18).

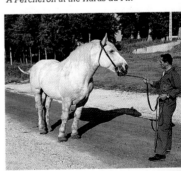

A Percheron at the Haras du Pin

♦♦♦
O, CHÂTEAU D' ✓

southeast of Argentan

A kind of French Elsinore, with its tall gatehouse and witch's hat roofs, the strangely named Château d'O stands beside a dreamy lake.

The building has much of the Renaissance about it, but the oldest part dates from the 15th century. To this, two newer wings were subsequently added round a courtyard. The effect is a harmonious and enchanting whole, and the interiors are well worth seeing too. Several members of the O family, the one-time owners, were prominent government figures of their day.

Open: daily, July to September.
Closed: February, and mornings from October to June.

You can picnic in the park or dine in the restaurant (tel: 33 35 35 27) in the stable block.

The stuff of fairy-tales – Château d'O, mirrored in its lake

♦

ORBEC

An attractive small town at the southern end of the Auge, Orbec has an assortment of appealing old houses in its busy main street, where a good range of everyday shops and a small country market can also be found. There are a couple of good hotel-restaurants: the **France**, 152 rue Grande (tel: 31 32 74 02), and **Au Caneton**, 32 rue Grande (tel: 31 32 73 32).

Tourist Office

rue Guillonière (tel: 31 32 87 15).

♦

PIN, LE

east of Argentan

Haras du Pin – the French National Stud – has been situated here since the time of Louis XIV. The château is not open, but the stables and carriage collection are.

Open: daily, (guided tours only). On Thursdays at 15.00hrs from mid-May to mid-September there is a parade of stallions.

PONT-AUDEMER

Though close to the Paris–Caen motorway and the industry of the lower Seine, Pont-Audemer is a quiet town full of charming back streets with half-timbered riverside houses and an 11th-century church, **St-Ouen**. The *pont* was for centuries the lowest bridge on the River Risle, and Pont-Audemer has long been a useful halting point for travellers. One further attraction is its thriving market which takes over the town Mondays and Fridays.

Between Pont-Audemer and the Pont de Tancarville is the low-lying country of the **Marais Vernier**. Especially attractive in spring, this little-known, rural corner of the Seine Valley is surrounded by some fine viewpoints – ideal for a last 'breath of French air' before travelling on to Le Havre.

Accommodation and Restaurants

Pont-Audemer's **Auberge du Vieux Puits**, 6 rue Notre-Dame-du-Pré (tel: 32 41 01 48) is a fine '*maison ancienne normande*' and a former tannery. Traditional dishes are served in welcoming surroundings, and guests have a choice of smaller, simpler bedrooms in the main building or more modern ones in the new wing.

Tourist Office

place Maubert (tel: 32 41 08 21).

PONTÉCOULANT

southwest of Clécy

This serene, mostly 18th-century château stands in an English-style park in the Suisse Normande – one of the few châteaux in the region.
Open: Wednesday to Monday.
Closed: October; mornings in winter.

ST-GABRIEL-BRÉCY

east of Bayeux

Only the east end remains of the ornate, late Romanesque priory church here, although the 13th-century gatehouse and the 14th-century prior's lodgings are intact. The priory is now a horticultural school whose gardens can also be visited.
Open: daily all year (guided tours July to September).

ST-GERMAIN-DE-LIVET

south of Lisieux

This splendid Renaissance château – one of the best in Normandy – evokes all the pageantry of a tournament, with its chequered walls and conical turrets. Surviving frescos of the late 16th century show battle scenes.
Open: Wednesday to Monday.
Closed: first half of October; mid-December to January.

ST-PIERRE-SUR-DIVES

southwest of Lisieux

The extraordinary market hall makes this ordinary, out-of-the-way little town worth visiting for its market alone. The great barn of a building, which now shelters chickens and rabbits on market days, was destroyed in 1944, but was later rebuilt. This was done using replicas of the medieval timbers and

dowels (of which there are said to be nearly 300,000) and no nails. A **museum of cheese-making** can be found in the former abbey.
Open: Wednesday to Monday.

Tourist Office
12 rue St Benoît (tel: 31 20 97 90).

◆

SASSY, CHÂTEAU DE
south of Argentan
This imposing 18th-century château with seigneurial views is still owned by the dukes of Audriffet-Pasquier, who were influential statesmen in the days of Louis-Philippe.
Open: gardens at all times; château Easter to October.

◆

SÉES
This small town was an important place in late Gallo-Roman antiquity, when it became a bishopric. It still has a bishop, and a medium-sized cathedral rebuilt during the 13th and 14th centuries. Some of the fine stained glass dates from the same period. There are pleasant hotels and restaurants for countryside tourers or ramblers in the nearby Forêt d'Ecouves.

Accommodation
An old favourite is the **Cheval Blanc**, a timber-and-plaster inn, 1 place St-Pierre (tel: 33 27 80 48); also recommended is the **Normandy**, 12 rue Ardrillers (tel:33 27 80 67), with an inexpensive restaurant.
A good country hotel is the **Ile de Sées**, three miles (5km) away at Macé on the D303 (tel: 33 27 98 65).

Tourist Office
Hôtel de Ville, place Général de Gaulle (tel: 33 28 74 79).

◆

THURY-HARCOURT
One of several centres for visiting the Suisse Normande, Thury-Harcourt is on the northern edge of the area beside the River Orne. The château was one of many buildings destroyed in 1944, though its chapel and park – now fully restored to include a series of gardens – survive.
Open: afternoons daily, June to September; Sundays and holidays May, June and October.

◆

VENDEUVRE, CHÂTEAU DE
southwest of St-Pierre-sur-Dives
The château was the work of the distinguished architect Jacques-François Blondel, but is an unexceptional design.

Vimoutiers – Marie Harel's statue

Besides the intact interiors and fine gardens, there is a museum of miniature furniture, featuring apprentices' 'masterpieces' or exercises to demonstrate their cabinet-working skills.
Open: afternoons daily, June to mid-September, weekend and holiday afternoons Easter to May and mid-September to October.

◆
VERNEUIL-SUR-AVRE
This one-time English stronghold in the southern Ouche region has little sign of its early history. The Flamboyant Gothic church of **La Madeleine** was rebuilt after Verneuil's final recapture by the French in 1449. The second church, **Notre-Dame**, has a notable series of 16th-century statues by local craftsmen. Verneuil is a good centre for touring or rambling.

Accommodation and Restaurants
There are a couple of good-value restaurant-hotels – the rather expensive **Hostellerie du Clos**, 98 rue Ferté-Vidame (tel: 32 32 21 81), and the excellent **Saumon**, 89 place Madeleine (tel: 32 32 02 36).

Tourist Office
129 place Madeleine (tel: 32 32 17 17).

◆
VIMOUTIERS
This is famous as the place where Camembert was first sold. Marie Harel, who brought it to the market here, made it in the neighbouring village of

Camembert. There is a Camembert museum just by the tourist office.
Open: Monday afternoon to Sunday.
Closed: Saturday afternoon and Sunday, November to April.
Vimoutiers is almost equally well known for its Calvados. Both are liberally offered for tasting in the town and on some of the nearby farms.

Tourist Office
10 avenue Général de Gaulle (tel: 33 39 30 29).

Exploring Camembert Country
Visitors to the Vimoutiers area of the Pays d'Auge will not escape reminders that this was the birthplace of this classic soft cheese.
Having visited the **Musée du Camembert** in Vimoutiers itself, you could seek out Marie Harel's home village (its name now a household word) just southwest of the town. Then why not drive along all or part of the **Route du Camembert**. Like the *Route des Fromages*, a little further north (taking in Livarot and Pont l'Evêque), the *Route du Camembert* is not only for cheese freaks. The drive should appeal to anyone who enjoys exploring the quintessential Normandy countryside of green pastures and orchards, tucked-away farmsteads and rural lanes. Tasting farm-produced cheeses, and perhaps buying some for a picnic lunch or to take home with you, is an added bonus along the way.

NORTHWEST NORMANDY: COTENTIN, *BOCAGE* AND MONT-ST-MICHEL

The northern half of the *département* of Manche forms the Cotentin Peninsula (also known in English as the Cherbourg Peninsula). Inland, much of the country here and further south is all of a piece with the neighbouring parts of middle Normandy known as the *Bocage*. It is a pleasant, varied countryside of hedgerows, meadows, orchards and woods, rich in wild flowers, with a few peaceful small market towns and historic abbeys.

The western coast of Manche, facing the Channel Islands, has many excellent beaches and unfashionable, uncrowded resorts that often have a refreshingly dated feel. This part of Normandy is a little too far from Paris for a comfortable day trip; other visitors also tend either to stop earlier or to travel further on to Brittany. However, it is quite easily accessible to the British, crossing the Channel to Cherbourg.

The southernmost stretch of this coast faces into the bay of Mont-St-Michel. Neighbouring Brittany forms most of the bay's southern and western edges, but tucked into its southeastern corner is a bit of Normandy that must not be missed – Mont-St-Michel itself. Visit early or late in the day: with up to three-quarters of a million visitors annually, this spectacular site is not a place to get away from the crowds.

By contrast, much of the northern Cotentin has a rather remote feel, and at the tip the character of its coastline changes. It is often compared to Brittany or Cornwall. Instead of flat strands, the coast rears up into storm-beaten cliffs, and it is a land of points and lighthouses, with a history of wrecks. Nevertheless the northeastern inland region known as the Val de Saire is pretty and friendly country. Here you are never far from the coast, which is punctuated by pleasant, quiet fishing villages. Further south, the flatter and rather featureless eastern seaboard has attracted much attention for its role – as Utah Beach – in the D-Day landings of 1944.

The upper Cotentin is sparsely populated except for the major industrial port of Cherbourg, which feels anything but remote. Next in size among the towns of Manche comes the historic but badly bombed St-Lô. These two modern towns have eclipsed the old capital, Coutances – which remains, however, one of the most agreeable towns in the whole of Normandy.

WHAT TO SEE

AVRANCHES
This has been a kind of landing-stage for Mont-St-Michel (see pages 85–6) ever since Aubert, Bishop of Avranches, was nudged rather violently by the angel Michael into founding the monastery there in the 8th century. You can look out to the Mount from the town and today, in summer, you can even go for a flight over it from Avranches'

little airfield. The **Musée de
l'Avranchin** in the former
bishop's palace has
manuscripts from Mont-St-
Michel, and an archaeological
and popular art section.
Open: Wednesday to Monday,
Easter to mid-October.

In its own right Avranches can
now boast perhaps only its
Jardins des Plantes (municipal
gardens), in which it outdoes
most other towns in the area,
though they compete. On the
site of the destroyed cathedral,
the spot is marked where
Henry II knelt to do penance for
the murder at Canterbury in
1170 of Thomas Becket. On
another preserved site the
American General Patton
stayed in 1944, at the time of the
so-called Avranches offensive
against the main German
Panzer division. There is a war
museum, **Musée de la Seconde**

*Not a plant out of place – the public
gardens in Avranches*

Guerre Mondiale, at **Le Val St-
Père**, to the south.
Open: daily, in summer;
weekends and holidays in
winter.

Accommodation
A number of small, reasonable
hotels make Avranches an
excellent stop for a tour
including Mont-St-Michel. **La
Croix d'Or**, 83 rue Constitution
(tel: 33 58 04 88) has newly
been splendidly refurbished. A
modern contrast is **Les
Abrincates**, 37 boulevard
Luxembourg (tel: 33 58 66 64),
or try the **Jardin des Plantes**, 10
place Carnot (tel: 33 58 03 68),
with good-value home cooking.

Tourist Office
2 rue Général de Gaulle (tel: 33
58 00 22).

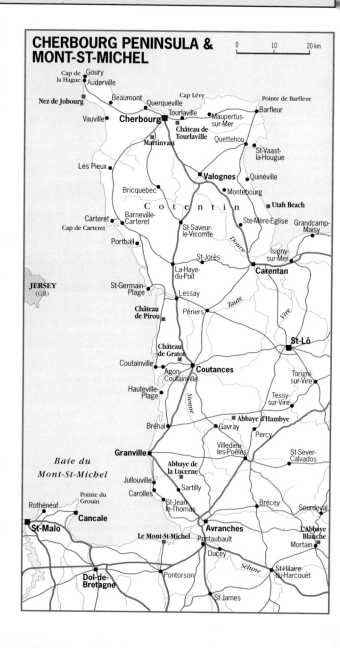

CHERBOURG PENINSULA & MONT-ST-MICHEL

0   10   20 km

Cap de la Hague
Goury
Auderville
Nez de Jobourg
Beaumont
Querqueville
Cap Lévy
Pointe de Barfleur
Tourlaville
Maupertus-sur-Mer
Barfleur
Vauville
Cherbourg
Château de Tourlaville
Quettehou
St-Vaast-la-Hougue
Martinvast
Les Pieux
Quinéville
Valognes
Montebourg
Bricquebec
C o t e n t i n
Utah Beach
Barneville-Carteret
Ste-Mère-Église
Grandcamp-Maisy
Carteret
Cap de Carteret
St-Saveur-le-Vicomte
Portbail
Douve
St-Jorès
Isigny-sur-Mer
JERSEY (GB)
La-Haye-du-Puit
Carentan
St-Germain-Plage
Lessay
Taute
Château de Pirou
Périers
Vire
St-Lô
Château de Gratot
Coutainville
Coutances
Torigni-sur-Vire
Agon-Coutainville
Tessy-sur-Vire
Hauteville-Plage
Sienne
Abbaye d'Hambye
Bréhal
Gavray
Percy
Granville
Abbaye de la Lucerne
Villedieu-les-Poêles
St-Sever-Calvados
Baie du Mont-St-Michel
Jullouville
Carolles
Sartilly
St-Jean-le-Thomas
Brécey
Sourdeval
Pointe du Grouin
Rothéneuf
Cancale
Avranches
L'Abbaye Blanche
St-Malo
Le Mont-St-Michel
Pontaubault
Mortain
Ducey
Séune
St-Hilaire-du-Harcouët
Dol-de-Bretagne
Pontorson
St-James

◆◆
BARFLEUR
east of Cherbourg

Barfleur is a romantic fishing-port and now a yachting marina. A stroll in its attractive and quiet streets offers a good first taste of France to visitors arriving at Cherbourg.

Barfleur was frequently used as a Channel port in Norman times and the White Ship, in which William Atheling (heir to Henry I) and his retinue drowned in 1120, foundered close by. The tragedy upset Henry's careful dynastic plans and gave rise, after his death, to the civil wars of Stephen and Matilda.

Today Barfleur has the tallest **lighthouse** in Normandy, for its waters are still dangerous, being shallow and with strong currents. The fit can climb its 365 steps for the view.
Open: daily, April to September; winter, Sundays only.

Accommodation
The best hotel is the simple **Conquérant**, 16–18 rue St-Thomas-Becket (tel: 33 54 00 82). Duke William is said to have set off from here for Dives on his way to conquer England.

Tourist Office
rue St-Thomas-Becket (tel: 33 54 02 48).

◆◆
BARNEVILLE-CARTERET

Barneville and Carteret lie on opposite sides of a sheltered harbour behind the point of Cap de Carteret. The amenities of these merged resorts include a port (departure point for the Channel Islands) and marina, cliffs with a walk, and two **beaches**. There is also an excellent **market**, for both sea and land produce.

In summer Barneville and Carteret swell with seasonal visitors, mostly French, staying close by on a traditional family holiday. The place is crowded enough for atmosphere, but not swamped, not pressured, and not smart.

Barneville's church is mostly Romanesque, with some notable carving on the arches and capitals.

Accommodation and Restaurants
There are quite a number of decent and reasonable places

Barfleur's historic fishing port

to stay and to eat. **Les Isles**, 9 boulevard Maritime, Barneville-Plage (tel: 33 04 90 76) is more of a family hotel, with straightforward cooking. The **Marine**, 11 rue de Paris, Carteret (tel: 33 53 83 31), is the grandest, with a starred restaurant.

Tourist Offices
Barneville – rue des Ecoles (tel: 33 04 90 58); Carteret – place Flandres-Dunkerque (tel: 33 04 94 54; April to September only).

BRICQUEBEC
inland, between Cherbourg and Barneville-Carteret
A remarkable 11-sided 14th-century *donjon* (keep) on a motte or mound dominates Bricquebec's ruined castle, which still also has its curtain wall and gatehouse.
Open: ruins at all times.
The big market place nearby hums into life on Monday mornings.

CARENTAN
Set at the foot of the Cotentin Peninsula, on the main route to Cherbourg, Carentan would benefit from a by-pass. People come here for the market, which specialises in cattle and for the yacht marina, a successful new attraction. The church of **Notre-Dame** has perhaps the most easterly piece of Flamboyant Gothic architecture in Normandy.

Accommodation
A good hotel and restaurant is the **Hotel du Commerce et de la Gare**, 34 rue de la Gare (tel: 33 42 02 00).

Tourist Office
Hôtel de Ville (tel: 33 42 05 87).

CAROLLES
south of Granville
Slightly inland, Carolles village is situated in pleasant walking country (for instance, the so-called **Vallée des Peintres** – Artists' Vale – or the **Vallée du Lude**). **Carolles-Plage** is an equally pleasant beach resort.

CARTERET see BARNEVILLE-CARTERET

CHERBOURG
There is something gloomy about most of the Channel ports – perhaps because nobody looks at them, or stays in them unless they are stuck there. Cherbourg is no exception. It is a big town, but deserves only a short description – even for restaurants it is not exceptional. Its streets look like Normandy, it has a market, it has bars and restaurants and hotels, but none of them seem to match what one finds inland.
Cherbourg had some importance between the Wars – when transatlantic liners regularly docked here – and during World War II, once the Battle of Normandy was over and it became the main port for Allied supplies. The **Musée de la Guerre et de la Libération** documents this role. Pictures in the modern **Musée des Beaux-Arts Thomas-Henry** include local landscapes (notably by the 19th-century painter of peasantry J-F Millet) and a small international collection.

Open: both museums
Wednesday to Monday.
Outside Cherbourg there is
much to see. Westwards lies
the rugged **La Hague**
peninsula, eastwards the **Val de
Saire**, pretty country giving on
to some charming harbours.
Out at **Querqueville** (off the
D901 up the Hague peninsula),
the little pre-Norman church of
St-Germain is something of a
curiosity. The trefoil plan and
patterned stonework recall
Early Christian or Byzantine
building.

Accommodation and Restaurants
There are chain hotels in
Cherbourg, and smaller,
ordinary ones. Reasonable
restaurants include **Le
Grandgousier**, 21 rue Abbaye
(tel: 33 53 19 43) and **Chez
Pain**, 59 rue au Blé (tel: 33 53
67 64).

Tourist Office
2 quai Alexandre-III (tel: 33 93
52 02).

◆
COUTAINVILLE
This is the *plage* (beach) for
Coutances inland, and more
than enough of it – miles of sand
and dunes on the exposed west
coast. Though it has some
modern facilities such as
windsurfing, Coutainville is still
not smart, but much more a
family holiday place. There are
several adequate places to stay
and to eat along the front.

Tourist Office
place 28 Juillet 1944 (tel: 33 47
01 46).

The clock tower at Carolles

◆◆◆
COUTANCES
The **cathedral**, still the
centrepiece of Coutances, is
one of the finest in Normandy,
and definitely the finest for a
long way around. Though
retaining its 11th-century plan,
foundations and piers, and even
the older western towers, it was
rebuilt in an Early Gothic style
after a fire in 1208. Despite the
constraints – which, for
instance, produced a narrow
chancel – the adaptation was
skilful, and was completed
within the 13th century
(including the windows) without
change of style. Only the spires
over the front and the crossing
towers are later, but equally
harmonious.
Open: daily, in summer; by
appointment in winter.
The town is little more than one
main street, giving on to quiet,

bourgeois back streets. There is quite an elaborate municipal garden and a small museum (**Musée Quesnel-Morinière**). *Open:* Wednesday to Monday. *Closed:* Wednesday, Sunday morning and holidays in winter. Coutances has few hotels or restaurants.

Tourist Office
place Georges-Leclerc (tel: 33 45 17 79).

◆◆
GRANVILLE
A lively place with several points of interest, Granville is primarily a summer resort, but is also known for its carnival or *mardi gras*. It takes on character not only from its fishing port and marina, but also from the cliffs of the **Pointe du Roc** and the surviving ramparts of the upper town, built by the English in the 15th century to threaten Mont-St-Michel.

The 'sights' range from the severe church of **Notre-Dame** to a peaceful public garden that once belonged to the family of Christian Dior, a waxworks museum (**Historial Granvillais**), a 'Palais Minéral', a 'Féerie de Coquillage' (shellwork extravaganza) and an aquarium . Such attractions have a Victorian, trip-to-the-pier ring, which is right for this old-fashioned but still thriving family resort.

Open: daily, summer only; Sundays and holidays in winter. You can see local artefacts and historical displays in the **Musée du Vieux Granville**.

Open: Wednesday to Monday April to September; winter weekends.

Boat trips are available out to the nearby **Iles Chausey** (Chausey Islands), with their 19th-century forts, and to the **Channel Islands**.

Accommodation
A really good, simple hotel is the **Michelet**, 5 rue Michelet (tel: 33 50 06 55); but there are others.

Restaurants
Several good eating places are another point in Granville's favour. **Le Phare**, 11 rue Port (tel: 33 50 12 94), is a packed favourite; also **Normandy-Chaumière**, 20 rue Poirier (tel: 33 50 01 71) and **La Gentilhommière**, 152 rue Couraye (tel: 33 50 17 99).

Tourist Office
4 cours Jonville (tel: 33 91 30 03).

The Abbaye de Hambye is off the beaten track, but worth findng

◆
GRATOT, CHÂTEAU DE
northwest of Coutances
This ruined château with its
moat and its crumbling towers
is delightfully picturesque. Only
the offset square tower goes
back to the 14th century, when
the castle is first recorded; the
other buildings date from the
15th or 18th centuries.
Open: daily, all year.

◆◆
HAGUE PENINSULA
northwest of Cherbourg
Reaching out towards the
Channel Islands, with views
over to them in fine weather,
the peninsula of La Hague is a
land of dry-stone walls, empty
heaths, wind, gulls and dour
granite rock. Between the **Cap
de la Hague** and the island of
Alderney, the Alderney Race is
rendered deadly by its very
swift currents; there is a heroic
lifeboat station at the tiny port of

Goury. Just south of the Cap,
the **Nez de Jobourg** presents a
memorable spectacle of raw
rock and foaming sea. There is
a walk along the western cliff,
from Goury south to **Vauville**.
Here a long, unspoilt beach
stretches away southwards,
backed by wild dunes. The
stone buildings of Vauville itself,
clustered round its stream,
include a 16th-century château
(not open).

◆◆
HAMBYE, ABBAYE DE
east of Granville
Hambye is one of the finest of
Normandy's many ruined
abbeys, partly because it is set
in beautiful countryside. Most of
the nave and chancel – dating
from the 13th and 14th
centuries – survive, though
roofless. The later outbuildings,
some of which are intact, house
furnishings and tapestries.
Open: Wednesday to Monday.
Closed: mid-December to
January.

Accommodation
The nearby **Auberge de
l'Abbaye** (tel: 33 61 42 19) is an
excellent country hotel.

◆
JULLOUVILLE
south of Granville
This is another of those
Normandy resorts where time
seems to have stood still. The
resort itself is small, with an
extensive suburb of pre-War
villas. It is a good place for
young children.

Tourist Office
avenue Maréchal Leclerc (tel:
33 61 82 48).

NORTHWEST NORMANDY

LESSAY
north of Coutances
The little town is dominated by its ex-abbey **church**, founded in 1056. The style is Romanesque but with rib vaults anticipating Gothic structures. The church is an exceptionally beautiful and rare example of a fairly large Romanesque church completed in one building programme. Not on the scale of St-Etienne in Caen, but larger than a normal parish church, it has three storeys inside but only two outside. Masked on the outside by the aisle roof, the intermediate storey is a 'false gallery'. Unroofed in 1944, the church has been meticulously restored and any later additions have been removed.
The nearby beaches to the west – long, broad and sandy – are undeveloped and almost deserted. They are wonderful for children – and molluscs.

LUCERNE, ABBAYE DE LA
southeast of Granville
The church of this ruined abbey, set in pleasant countryside, dates from the 12th century, and is transitional between Romanesque – a rather heavily decorated late Romanesque portal survives – and Gothic, for instance the tower over the transept. Not all the ruins are so old: the cloister is, but the ruined aqueduct was built in 1803 for a mill installed in the grounds.
Open: daily, mid-March to mid-November; weekends and school holidays rest of year.
Closed: January.

The Normans and Romanesque Architecure
Although the Normans did not exactly invent Romanesque – a term usually used to describe a manner of building prevalent all over Europe in the 11th and 12th centuries – they certainly evolved a new variation, important not only in itself but also because it led directly to the development of the Gothic style. The most important forebear of the new vaulting system essential to Gothic architecture is the late 11th-century Norman Cathedral at Durham in England, but there are also contemporary signs in mainland Normandy of the new use of rib vaulting, for instance here at Lessay or in the lowest chambers of the twin towers of Bayeux Cathedral. Here we find cemented rubble vaults sustained not only by arches round the sides of the square, but also by great ribs crossing its diagonals. With the arrival of the Gothic style, ribs such as these became the basis of the whole vaulting system.

MARTINVAST
southwest of Cherbourg
The château here is a rambling, cobbled medieval castle updated in the Renaissance and then again in the 19th century. It is a fine backdrop for an extensive arboretum.
Open: afternoons at weekends and public holidays. Special events include a *son et lumière* in summer.

◆◆◆
MONT-ST-MICHEL ✓

Mont-St-Michel is a unique and memorable experience, a 'must'. No photograph can capture the drama that unfolds when you see it for the first time. As you approach it, the landscape changes completely. Empty, marshy flats give way to the bare strand itself and the sea. Several hundred yards (metres) from the shore, the extraordinary granite island rises from the watery levels, its steepness accentuated by the spire of the abbey church at the top.

Unmissable Mont-St-Michel

The rock is not large, but can seem extraordinarily isolated, despite the modern causeway that links it to the mainland. Around it the tide comes in very fast – and deep – so an awareness of the tide table is an elementary caution (especially if you park in the lower car park).

Mont-St-Michel has a long history. The 'Michel' is Michael the Archangel, an important saint of the Carolingian era. Mont-St-Michel is one of several European shrines to him that date back to the Middle Ages. All of them are built on rocks where the angel was said to have appeared.

Architecturally, Mont-St-Michel is a hotch-potch of dates, styles and uses, from the 9th to the 19th centuries, and from place of pilgrimage to prison. Religious, domestic and military buildings sit cheek by jowl, and a tour involves a bewildering sequence of steps, passages, open spaces and rooms.

High above the ramparts, the abbey buildings are well worth the strenuous climb. The earliest church on the site was converted into a crypt when the larger Romanesque church was built in the 11th and 12th centuries. Of this church the nave remains; the chancel was replaced in the 15th and 16th centuries in the Flamboyant style. Sadly, the old Romanesque façade and the last three bays of the nave were destroyed in the 19th century. The finest architecture of the abbey is the part known as La Merveille, built by King Philip Augustus between 1211 and 1228, and opening off the north side of the church. On its topmost level the Merveille consists of a very beautiful cloister (often only to be peeped at, not entered) and a refectory; beneath there are a couple of large halls, and cellars. This was the guest wing, which had to be worthy of visiting kings, and the overall effect of Philip Augustus's Gothic is indeed dazzling. On the south side of the church are the buildings for the monks themselves, later in date and not so ornate. Beneath are several crypts. The superstructure of the church, including the spire, is late 19th-century. Ramparts and gardens surround the immediate precinct of the abbey.

Open: abbey church, cloister and refectory daily except some public holidays, by guided tour only.

It is not surprising that, as Normandy's most famous sight, Mont-St-Michel becomes very crowded in summer (especially during the several festivals). Cars and coaches pack the car parks at the end of the causeway, their occupants choosing either just to stop and stare, or to follow the crowds toiling up through the ramparts on foot. Restaurants, souvenir shops and other tourist attractions line the Grande Rue – the steep main thoroughfare leading up to the abbey.

There are three museums – designed more for entertainment than for instruction. The **Archéoscope** is full of high-tech devices explaining the history of Mont-St-Michel. The **Musée Grévin** offers a series of tableaux with waxwork figures of people associated with the Mount through the ages. The **Musée de la Mer** contains local marine curiosities and gives film presentations on the tidal peculiarities of the bay.

Open: all three museums daily, February to mid-November.

The abbey is illuminated every evening at nightfall. During the summer season it is the setting for *son et lumière* shows, every evening except Sunday.

There are those who claim that Mont-St-Michel is best visited out of season. Certainly it is more atmospheric when free of the summer hubbub. However, it can be bleak in winter, and some of the hotels, restaurants and shops may be closed.

Accommodation and Restaurants

As in most tourist traps, the hotels, restaurants and shops on Mont-St-Michel do not offer very good value. However, there are a dozen or so hotel-restaurants to choose from, and staying the night offers the advantage of being here in the evening and early morning when day-trippers are few. The disadvantage is that you must carry your luggage up from the car park at the bottom.

The famous restaurant **Mère Poulard**, Grande Rue (tel: 33 60 14 01), has declined from its former glory, although it is still good, if expensive. (Mère Poulard was famous at the beginning of the century for her omelettes, and the restaurant still is.) A large place with a large turnover, the **Terrasses Poulard**, Grande Rue (tel: 33 60 14 09), offers perhaps the best available. Both are hotels as well as restaurants. The **Saint Pierre**, Grande Rue (tel: 33 60 14 03), has attractive bedrooms and a busy, informal restaurant.

Tourist Office

Corps du Gard de Bourgeois (entrance) (tel: 33 60 14 30).

Milestone on 'Liberty Way' at Utah Beach, near Ste-Mère-Eglise

 ◆◆
PIROU, CHÂTEAU DU
southwest of Lessay
This rather shambling but charming castle dates from the 12th century with considerable internal modifications. It still has its moat, its curtain wall and a number of gatehouses, but has lost its keep. A modern 'imitation' of the Bayeux tapestry displayed in one of the rooms tells the story of the local Hauteville family, who conquered Sicily and South Italy in 1071 – a story every bit as dramatic as William the Conqueror's.
Open: afternoons daily; also mornings in July and August.
Closed: Tuesday out of season.

 ◆
ST-LÔ
St-Lô's history goes back to Roman times, but the town suffered heavily when it was bombed in 1944 as a key strongpoint. It also suffered when it was rebuilt. The ruins of the church of **Notre-Dame**, which was not reconstructed,

are a telling illustration of the damage that was caused.
A set of 16th-century tapestries is the highlight of the small collection in the **Musée Municipal des Beaux-Arts**.
Open: Wednesday to Monday.
South of St-Lô, in the valley of the Vire, there are beauty spots such as the **Roches de Ham**, a cliff above the winding river.

Accommodation
The town has perfectly good places to stay and to eat, all with a modern ambience. Among the several modest hotels is the **Hotel des Voyageurs**, place Gare (tel; 33 05 08 63), incorporating the **Marignan** restaurant (tel: 33 05 15 15).

Tourist Office
2 rue Havin (tel: 33 05 02 09).

 ◆◆
STE-MÈRE-EGLISE
between Valognes and Carentan
The simple farming village of Ste-Mère-Eglise is the largest settlement in the rather featureless rural area north of Carentan. It has an early Gothic church and a farm museum, the **Ferme-Musée du Cotentin**.
Open: Wednesday to Monday, Easter to September (daily, July and August); also open weekend afternoons in October.
Ste-Mère-Eglise will be remembered by many as the scene of fierce fighting in 1944, when airborne troops were dropped to supplement the efforts of the US Army landing on the long expanse of 'Utah Beach' to the east. The events of this period are commemorated in the **Musée des Troupes Aéroportées** (Airborne Troops

Museum). There is another war museum (**Musée du Débarquement à Utah-Beach**) at **Ste-Marie-du-Mont**, to the southeast.
Open: both museums daily in summer.
Closed: mid-November to January.

ST-SAUVEUR-LE-VICOMTE
southwest of Valognes
The remains of a powerful castle here include a 14th-century keep declared at the time to be 'impregnable to both machine and assault'. An older round keep and some of the bailey's outbuildings also survive.
Open: at all times.

ST-VAAST-LA-HOUGUE
northeast of Valognes
Though it has not quite the appeal of Barfleur, to the north (see page 79), St-Vaast-la-Hougue is an attractive fishing-port and resort with the remains of 17th-century fortifications – notably the **Fort de la Hougue** (not open), at the end of the long promontory known as the Grande-Plage.

Accommodation and Restaurants
A pleasant, well-run simple hotel and restaurant is the **France et Fuchsias**, 18 rue Maréchal Foch (tel: 33 54 42 26). There are some newly converted bedrooms in the annexe at the bottom of the pretty garden. Another is the **Granitière**, 64 rue Maréchal Foch (tel: 33 54 58 99). There are several good fish restaurants by the harbour.

Tourist Office
Quai Vauban (tel: 33 54 41 37).

TOURLAVILLE, CHÂTEAU DE
east of Cherbourg
Conveniently close to Cherbourg, this late 16th-century château may be worth visiting to pass the time while waiting for a ferry, rather than for its architectural merit. It was left to ruin and then so restored in the 19th century that nothing authentic remains. However, swans swim in its lily-covered lake, and it has an arboretum.
Open: daily.

VALOGNES
A straightforward market town, Valognes suffered terrible war damage in 1944. Its **Hôtel de Beaumont**, however, is an 18th-century building with a fine staircase and some good surviving furnishings.
Open: afternoons daily, Easter weekend and July to mid-September.
The history of cider-making in Normandy is explored in the **Musée régional du cidre**.
Open: Thursday to Tuesday, Easter holiday and June to September.
Closed: Sunday mornings.

Accommodation and Restaurants
Valognes offers a choice of good hotel-restaurants. The best known is the **Louvre**, 28 rue Réligieuses (tel: 33 40 00 07); or try **Hôtel de l'Agriculture**, 16 rue Léopold-Delisle (tel: 33 95 02 02). Both offer good meals.

Tourist Office
place Château (tel: 33 40 11 55).

Peace and Quiet

*Countryside and Wildlife
in Normandy
by Paul Sterry*

Above all, Normandy is green. Its setting in the cool, moist northwest of France is clearly of paramount influence here, but the greenness is, if anything, intensified by traditional agricultural practices, which encourage pastures and orchards. So the predominant 'feel' of Normandy as you travel through it is of a gentle place with venerable half-timbered farmsteads tucked away along tracks lined by equally venerable apple and pear trees. It all seems very slow and unhurried, but looks can be deceptive. This quiet landscape is actually very carefully tended, as you will realise if you look in the farmyards, nearly all of which have huge, neat stacks of firewood gathered from the hedgerow trees. (The reason that some of those trees look odd is that all of their lower branches are stripped off regularly as part of the wood-gathering process.) For many people, the best time to visit Normandy is in the spring, when the blossom is out and when the meadows and roadside verges are carpeted in wild flowers. This is also the time for bird song.

There are variations on the theme of peaceful greenness. Normandy's most 'rugged' inland landscapes are in the Suisse Normande (Norman Switzerland). However don't expect ski lifts or cloud-shrouded peaks. This is a landscape very much in the Normandy mould, but with river gorges and steepish hills.

A splendid, natural gateway to the forest at Château d'Harcourt

PEACE AND QUIET

There are extensive forests throughout the region, but many of these consist of youngish trees. All are carefully managed, so glades of ancient gnarled trees are few and far between. Often, these forests are on poor, acid soils, so the ground flora is likely to consist of such plants as heathers – good for insects and for reptiles. Normandy still has some areas of open heath and these are well worth seeking out for their bird and insect life. And then, of course, there is the seaside – miles of sandy beaches, often backed by sand dunes. There are also dramatic cliffs, the equal of any on the north European seaboard. Described below are some of Normandy's best areas for scenery and for wildlife, but almost any walk or cycle-ride along quiet, leafy lanes will bring pleasures and rewards.

Vauville Dunes

South of Vauville, on the Cotentin coast due west of Cherbourg, lies an extensive system of west-facing sand dunes, built up by surging Atlantic breakers. This is one of the best areas in Normandy for coastal flowers, with several unusual species. Insects also abound and migrant birds can often be found in the dune slacks (the damp areas in the hollows between the dunes). The pools attract ducks and other wildfowl, while in the reedbeds warblers and buntings may be seen. To reach the dunes, head west from Cherbourg and turn south at Beaumont for Vauville. At the village, turn off on the D237 and turn right to park by the campsite. Walk past the nature reserve sign and follow the path southwards.

Exciting and colourful flowers can be found from April until September, although in a dry summer many of the plants may wither by August. One of the most intriguing of the early species is dwarf pansy. The flower is just like a garden pansy, but the whole plant including the flower is minute – often less than one inch (2cm) high. Not surprisingly it can be difficult to locate.

Later in the season, Jersey thrift and spiked speedwell appear among the tussocks of marram grass. Wet, marshy areas harbour marsh orchids and other rare plants.

Colourful butterflies abound and great green bush crickets sing loudly. These large, bright green insects can be recognised by their long legs and long antennae. Their colouring, however, gives them good camouflage.

Seawatching

Especially in autumn, seabirds often stream past this headland, particularly in northwesterly gales. The birds are heading south from their breeding grounds further north in Europe to wintering quarters off southern Europe and Africa. Look for gannets – large, pure white birds – and several species of gulls and seaducks. Shearwaters, which fly on stiffly held wings, also fly by in large groups known as 'rafts'. Keen-eyed observers may even spot the occasional dolphin.

Cap de la Hague

For bracing walks and spectacular views, the stretch of north-facing Cotentin coastline between Urville-Nacqueville and Cap de la Hague is hard to beat. To reach the Cap de la Hague, drive west on the D901 to Auderville and then take the D401 northwards.

Cap de Flamanville

Cap de Flamanville, on the west coast mid-way between Cap de la Hague and Carteret, offers further spectacular walks with a chance to see interesting coastal flowers as well. Park at the *Sémaphore*, signposted off the minor road from Flamanville to Bonnemains. Walk south along the road, then down the path to the cliff edge. The walk southwards is particularly fine. It eventually leads back to the road, from where you can return to your car.

Thrift, also aptly known as sea pink, grows here in the spring and produces a carpet of pink flowers. It contrasts with the intense green of clumps of Portland spurge and, in places, gives the effect of a man-made rockery. Later in the season, sea lavender puts on a colourful show on the rock ledges.

Cap de Carteret

This is another part of the Cotentin's west coast that will appeal to anyone interested in coastal flowers. Pass through the village of Carteret and on to Cap de Carteret. The Cap overlooks Havre de Carteret, another good spot for spring flowers, which can be reached from Barneville-Carteret.

Cap Lévy to Phare de Gatteville

The northern Cotentin coastline between Cap Lévy and Gatteville-le-Phare east of Cherbourg is perhaps the most interesting stretch in Normandy for those most interested in coastal flowers and seabirds. Almost anywhere can be good and the best approach is to drive along the D116 between Fermanville and Gatteville, taking minor roads north to the coast. There is parking by the shore at the end of most of these roads.

The best areas are north of Renouville and Rethoville. At le Bas de la Rue there are coastal pools and marshes on the landward side of the shingle beach as you walk towards Gatteville. Wetland birds can

Sea spurge – a typical dune plant

PEACE AND QUIET

Watch for fan-tailed warblers in the marshes east of Gatteville

be found here and fan-tailed warblers are also common. These tiny birds are most easily recognised by the characteristic display of the male: his song is a continuous 'zip-zip-zip' delivered in a song flight where he looks as though he is suspended on a yo-yo.

The shoreline along this stretch grades from shingle to coarse sand, and a wide variety of flowers can be found here. Perhaps the most distinctive is sea holly, with leaves and flowers of purple grey. The leaves are extremely spiny and just like those of their namesake tree. Its close relative, field eryngo, also grows here. It too is a very spiny plant, but the leaves are altogether more slender in appearance. Other botanical specialities of this shoreline include cottonweed, whose stems and leaves are cloaked in downy hairs, and purple spurge. The latter is a prostrate plant with fleshy leaves and a purplish stem. Both purple spurge and cottonweed are declining species in other parts of northern Europe.

Coastal Plants
The Cotentin coast is a superb area to see coastal flowers. Most of the plants that grow by the sea are specially adapted to life in this difficult environment. They must be able to tolerate drying sea breezes and constant exposure to salt-laden air. In addition, many coastal plants live in a shifting environment of sand or shingle. Consequently, they often grow long or spreading root systems to keep them anchored and to reach water. The most characteristic plant of sand dunes is marram grass. In fact, it is among the first plants to colonise shifting sand, encouraging the dunes to become stable. Sea spurge and yellow horned-poppy are also colonists of the sand dunes and have extensive root systems.

Rocky Outcrops of la Glacerie

The landscape around la Glacerie and le Mesnil-au-Val, to the south of Cherbourg and Tourlaville, is rolling, with small fields, thick hedges and pockets of rich woodland. Additional interest is provided by the rocky outcrops which can be found in the area. Many support a rich growth of moisture-loving plants including ferns, and some are so covered in vegetation that they have ceased to look like rocks at all. To reach the area, drive south from Cherbourg on the N13 and then turn off east towards la

Woodland Birds

Spring is the season to look and listen for woodland birds in Normandy. From March to June, the woods are alive with song, those of resident species being supplemented by migrant visitors. Tits, warblers, finches and thrushes all vie with each other and it would not be unusual to see or hear 10 or more species in a single location. The warblers are perhaps the best woodland songsters. Listen for wood warblers which have a song with a distinctive trill. Blackcaps, males of which do indeed have black caps, have rich, melodious songs, while that of the nightingale is renowned both for its volume and for its variety and range. In addition, there are less conspicuous species such as short-toed treecreepers and woodpeckers to look out for.

White-letter Hairstreak

Because its foodplant, elm, has declined in northern Europe as a result of Dutch elm disease, the white-letter hairstreak – an attractively marked butterfly – has also suffered. However, in Normandy, many of the elms have survived attack, so this is a very good area to look for hairstreaks. The butterflies are on the wing in July and August and generally remain faithful to the particular tree on which they fed as caterpillars. Look for them flying around the highest branches on sunny days. When brambles are in flower, however, they can be easier to see: they descend to ground level to feed on the rich supply of nectar that the flowers produce.

Glacerie after a few miles. From there, several minor roads wind their way to le Mesnil-au-Val and on southwards to the D56. Explore any suitable patches of woodland and rocky outcrops, being careful not to leave gates open and not to disturb livestock.

Plants of particular interest to look out for among the rocky outcrops include Tunbridge filmy fern, a delicate, membranous species that forms quite large patches over rocks where water trickles down. The same habitat is also suitable for Cornish moneywort, so-called because the round leaves resemble coins, and ivy-leaved bellflower, which produces delicate mauve flowers in the early summer.

PEACE AND QUIET

Spring Hedgerow Flowers

In early spring, the hedgerows are full of colourful flowers. The reasons for the profusion of plant life lie in the lack of intensive farming in the surrounding fields and in the way in which the hedges are cut. In April and May, large yellow patches of primroses can be seen growing with clumps of early purple orchids and greater stitchwort among them. Where damp patches and ditches are to be found, look for the delicate white flowers of meadow saxifrage, a plant that cannot tolerate too much disturbance, and yellow splashes of opposite-leaved golden saxifrage.

Cowslips are also common, but are none the less extremely beautiful.

Forêt de St-Sauveur

St-Sauveur-le-Vicomte lies in the centre of the Cotentin Peninsula with the Forêt de St-Sauveur to its west. To reach it, drive west from St-Sauveur-le-Vicomte on the D15 and shortly take the right fork of the D130. This runs along the edge of the forest where you can park and explore the broadleaved woodland edge.

Bois de Limors

This area of woodland lies southeast of St-Sauveur-le-Vicomte and can be reached by taking the D900 south from the town and turning east after a few miles to Varenguebec. The woodland lies north of the road. Look for birds of prey circling overhead and listen for woodland birds in spring.

Lessay

South of Lessay – still in the Cotentin, between St-Sauveur and Coutances – lie some of the most extensive areas of heathland left in the Normandy

Perennial centaury, a coastal plant tolerant of wind and poor soil

Summer lady's tresses is becoming rare throughout Europe

region. To reach them, drive south from Lessay on the D2 for a few miles until you reach the heathland habitat. There are several stopping-off points along the main road as well as side roads. One good area is off the minor road which runs eastwards to La Feuillie. Here you can park the car and explore. Birdlife includes hobbies – small, aerobatic birds of prey – Dartford warblers and stonechats; several interesting species of plants grow here, too. The heaths are dominated by bell heather and ling; heath lobelia – similar to many garden varieties – is still common here, although it is a declining species in many other parts of Europe.

Summer Lady's Tresses

Summer lady's tresses is an intriguing species of orchid that grows on the heathlands of Lessay. It gains its name from the time of year of its appearance – summer – and the resemblance of the flower spike to a woven and twisted braid of hair. It has suffered a dramatic decline in its distribution throughout Europe and has become extinct in many areas. However, small colonies still persist in Normandy, although for how much longer it is difficult to predict. Summer lady's tresses has very precise habitat requirements and any change in land use could mean its certain disappearance.

PEACE AND QUIET

St-Germain-sur-Ay
The coast to the south of St-Germain-sur-Ay offers good opportunities for observing coastal birds. The village lies to the west of Lessay. Drive on the D650 coast road and turn off south through the village to reach the shore. In the summer months, look for terns and gulls while in autumn and winter brent geese, wigeon and other ducks can be seen.

Baie du Grand Vey
On the eastern side of the Cotentin Peninsula, this large estuary is an excellent place for coastal birds. It can be viewed on the west side from minor roads leading from Pouppeville and on the east side from minor roads off the D514 between Grandcamp-Maisy and Isigny. Autumn and winter are the best seasons, when thousands of wildfowl and waders may be seen.

Parc Régional de Brotonne
This extensive area of forest is sited in the meanders of the River Seine to the west of Rouen. It is criss-crossed with roads and tracks from surrounding towns and villages such as Bourneville, Hauville and Caudebec-en-Caux. Associated with the Forêt de Brotonne are a craft centre in Bourneville and a recreational centre at le Mesnil, near Jumièges. The woodland is good for birds and flowers in spring and early summer. Fungi are abundant in the autumn.

Great green bush cricket

Practical

This section (with the yellow band) includes food, drink, shopping, accommodation, nightlife, tight budget, special events etc

FOOD AND DRINK

If one word could sum up Normandy food, it would be 'rich' – rich in the good sense of abundant and various, but also in the not-so-good one of high in calories, or not easily digestible – for example in the alcoholic cream sauce known as *sauce Normande*. It may well not seem the place to go to improve your waistline, because Normandy is known above all for its butter and cheese, its cider and Calvados liqueur. However, the region deserves to be just as well known for its fish (the *sole Normande*) and shellfish, which are low in calories, and its farms produce yoghurt, *crème fraîche* and skimmed milk as well as thick cream and full-fat cheese.

Traditional Fare

Although in the larger cities more cosmopolitan food – from pizza to Chinese meals – is not hard to find, one of the remarkable things about Normandy restaurants and markets is the way they have stuck to tradition. Even Normandy's first-class,

Michelin-starred restaurants seldom subscribe to modern schools of cooking, but prefer to perfect traditional recipes, such as *canard rouennais* (Rouen duck). Also against the modern trend are the many offal dishes favoured in Normandy, from *tripe à la mode de Caen* to the *boudin noir* (black pudding) for which Mortagne-au-Perche is known. The traditionalism is often emphasised by the *'ancienne maison Normande'* (old Norman house) décor, more often genuine than not. The ideal pursued time and again is that of the old-fashioned hostelry or coaching inn; Normandy restaurants are very often true inns, with bedrooms. Normandy's expanses of green pasturage provide good meat of all cuts and most varieties – pork and chicken, as well as beef (though the French prefer their lamb imported from England), not to mention guinea fowl and lots of game. Meals are square and solid: hence the so called *trou Normand* (Norman hole), originally a bolt of Calvados taken during the meal to 'bore a hole' in a full stomach so as to take more on board. Nowadays it is a much less gross Calvados-flavoured sorbet, but the principle remains. Plates are piled high.

Fish and Shellfish

For seafood, Brittany is a rival, and the fish available in Normandy is caught in international seas, so can be matched elsewhere. Nevertheless, the fish everywhere is fresh and good, especially turbot, brill, mackerel and sole. The local shellfish, however, is virtually unbeatable. Superb are the pink and grey *crevettes* (shrimps), the several varieties of crab, the *moules* (mussels) especially, also the whelks and other molluscs if they appeal. Then there are the oysters, and the lobsters and crayfish of course. These can be obtained on the promenade beside beaches and on the quay of every port, and they will always be fresh and delicious. A normal 'pub lunch' in Normandy is cheap and wholesome *moule-frite* (mussels and chips). There are several traditional fish soup recipes, and these again can be a meal in themselves.

Normandy's Cheeses

Camembert, the most famous of Normandy cheeses, was invented at the beginning of the 19th century, and sold at the market in Vimoutiers in the Auge (see page 75). But there is an enormous variety of other Normandy cheeses. Most are of the soft (*matière grasse*) variety, creamy and bland when young,

shrunken and smelly when aged. The best known, such as Pont-l'Evêque, are now mass-produced and vary in quality. Rather than pursue any particular type, it is probably best to choose what looks best on the day and is ripe in the way you like it. Incidentally, Petit-Suisse is a Norman cheese, not Swiss – it was first made by an immigrant Swiss in the Bray region. Try it with summer fruit, such as strawberries or peaches, and a sprinkling of sugar.

Cider and Calvados

Cidre fermier is a long way from sweet, fizzy mass-produced cider; true Normandy cider can be a very manly drink. But it is also a very pleasant drink, ideal for a break in a café on a hot day. The same may be said of Pommeau, which is the Norman equivalent of Champagne. *Poiré* – the equivalent of cider made from pears – is common in the *Bocage* region.

Calvados can vary from the ordinary – the working man's breakfast, taken with his coffee – to the very special, aged and prized and very expensive. Both cider and Calvados are commonly drunk in Normandy instead of wine; they are not mere 'tourist' specialities, as the liqueur Bénédictine, invented long ago by the monks of Fécamp, perhaps is.

Restaurants

As already mentioned, the typical Norman restaurant is an inn, offering substantial, local, traditional fare in a half-timbered setting (preferably 500 years old). Generally

speaking, these establishments are very good – except sometimes in very heavily visited areas. The restaurants named in this guide are usually of this kind. Many of them are not cheap, but they consistently offer good (or even very good) value, compared with what you might pay in other countries or in other parts of France. Special notice must be taken of the fish restaurants that abound in Normandy's ports and along their beaches. So often the freshness of the fish or shellfish is more important than the cooking, and in these places you can seldom go wrong. Depending on the kind of fish you eat, some of these restaurants can also be very cheap. There are smarter fish restaurants, of course, including some of the best in France. The very best in quality is generally to be found in Normandy's larger cities, especially Rouen and Caen.

Where to begin?

Recommendations

The restaurants recommended in this guide are in most cases well established and tried and tested. Many of them are above average in quality and in price – the sort of place to go for a special occasion rather than for an ordinary meal. It is definitely advisable to book, or at least to get there early for lunch or dinner, at all of them. French restaurant meal times are generally lunch from 12.00 to 14.00hrs, and dinner from 19.00 to 21.30hrs. Most close one day a week and annually for two or three weeks' holiday, frequently for part of the high season if they are not on the coast (in Rouen, for instance), so that should be checked on the telephone, too. Do not worry if your French is poor; basic English is usually understood in such places. To pick out and list everyday

FOOD AND DRINK

places to eat would be lengthy and largely pointless, since you can eat well at a reasonable price virtually anywhere in Normandy. The region abounds in restaurants; all you have to do is to study the menu displayed outside, and go in. While some are better than others, very few are really bad. Even in the most popular tourist resorts at the height of the season, the food usually remains decent, even though prices rise and getting a table can become a struggle.

In summer, a number of farmers' wives will cook for tourists as well as for their families. An *ad hoc* restaurant of this kind is called a *ferme auberge*. Some are so well frequented that they are open virtually every night; others are discreet, and all you will see is a notice on the gatepost as you speed by. It is well worth stopping, and either telephoning or calling at the farm to make an appointment and decide a menu. The meal will invariably be delicious, and will probably be washed down with the Pommeau or Calvados the farmer makes himself. It will be much more than you can eat, and very good value.

In season the seaside resorts abound with fast-food outlets: these will seldom be branded but local and individual and the *frites* (chips) are often very good – not to mention the pancakes from the *crêperies* and the *gauffres* (waffles) which the French seem to flock to eat about the middle of the afternoon.

Lunch 'en plein air' in Honfleur

SHOPPING

Markets

The best shopping in Normandy is for food, and the markets are irresistible. They are mostly food (especially vegetable) markets, but virtually anything can be sold. Every town and big village in Normandy has its market-day (often more than once a week). It is more exactly half a day, for the stalls are invariably closing up by lunchtime. They are filled not only by professional retailers but by many farmers or farmers' wives who are bringing their own produce for sale. Increasingly, farmers have become more imaginative and competitive. Despite CAP (the EU's farming subsidy), despite the many farms at which the lorries of large companies in the food industry draw up daily to remove the herd's entire output, some Normandy farmers have got the organic message and are making really tasty cheese again. Not so long ago it was beginning to seem that, in the land where Camembert was invented, mass-produced cheese was going to become the only sort available. But you will find home-made cheese at the market, as well as bottles of home-made cider and Calvados, besides a great variety of really fresh and often unusual vegetables. Hardware stalls offer good basic kitchen tools and handy gadgets such as oyster knives, or a screw-funnel you insert into a lemon you wish to squeeze (the juice comes tidily down the funnel while the lemon remains intact and can be used again).

Fish markets are usually specially designated, roofed structures. However, fish can frequently also be bought on the quay, when the boat comes in in the evening. At fish markets, each and every stall seems alive with comatose crabs and tetchy lobsters with their claws in rubber bands. Shellfish can often be bought ready cooked, and oysters will be opened for you. If you do buy fish, the messy preparation will be done while you wait. You will see ice used for packing, but never anything frozen.

Food Shops

The markets are complemented by delicatessens and specialist shops. As elsewhere in France, every town has at least one delicatessen where, if you could afford it, you could buy endless delicious prepared dishes and never have to cook. The *boulangeries* (bread) and *pâtisseries* (cakes) are good in Normandy, too. (*Boulangeries* are open on Sunday mornings, but are closed one day during the week – commonly Monday.) Besides these, you will find specialist cheese shops, excellent fishmongers, and butchers or *traiteurs* – which specialise in cold meats and sausages. Many such shops have a *rôtisserie* outside with chickens revolving on a spit in a greasy glass case: do not despise these, for the chickens will usually have ranged very freely and are delicious.

SHOPPING

Shop opening hours are generally from 08.β0 or 09.00hrs to 12.00 or 12.30hrs; then from about 14.00 or 14.30hrs until 19.00 or 19.30hrs. For more details, see **Opening Times**, page 121.

Supermarkets and Hypermarkets

Supermarkets (*supermarchés*) can be more convenient and in many cases just as good or nearly as good as traditional shops. In particular, their fruit and vegetables will rival those of the greengrocers, if not the market, and they will have a good delicatessen counter. But be warned that they will seldom be significantly cheaper. If you do not wish to shop every day, then it will be worth driving to a *hypermarché* outside town, where, in theory, everything you could wish to buy is gathered under one aeroplane-hangar roof.

The *hypermarchés* can be cheaper for certain things – in particular wine. Wine is not one of Normandy's native products and the quality of its wine-shops is generally low. Even Calvados and cider are better obtained at the *hypermarchés* or the day-markets than at wine shops. Things like children's clothes and toys, even bicycles, can be found at very competitive prices in the *hypermarchés*. They also sell cheaper petrol, though you usually have to queue. *Hypermarchés* remain open all day, often until 21.00 or 22.00hrs, but are closed on Sunday, and sometimes on Monday mornings too.

Other Shops

There are smart shops and department stores in the capitals, Caen and Rouen, and also – perhaps smartest of all – in Deauville. Otherwise, Normandy is the opposite of fashionable. However, its shops are hard to beat for basic, good-value everyday purchases. There are excellent chandlers and fishing shops, and the

Shop early at the market – most stalls pack up at lunchtime

French *quincaillerie* is a wonderful institution. It is usually translated as ironmonger, but it will sell a much wider range of goods, including tableware, light-bulbs and mosquito-killers.

These shops usually keep the same hours as food shops. Some, especially clothes shops, commonly remain closed on Monday morning.

Many newsagents verge on bookshops, and sell guides and maps, also some of the enormous range of French adult comics, which you will perhaps be glad your children cannot understand. Souvenir shops, usually concentrating on pottery, abound at seaside resorts. A certain type of blue and white lobed bowl, a little too small to be useful, with an individual Christian name, is positively ubiquitous.

ACCOMMODATION

Hotels

French hotels are generally cheap, depending on the exchange rate, and sometimes real bargains. This is true even of the national or international chains, though their tendency is to force up the prices towards the kind of sum businessmen are used to paying elsewhere. Nevertheless, an independent tourer staying for two weeks in hotels will run up a fearsome bill, one that most families will not begin to afford. Fortunately, there are many other ways of staying in Normandy (see below). But hotels are eminently practicable for a weekend, a stopover or a short stay. If you have children it is always worth asking for a family room, with three or four beds. Payment is by the room, not the person.

Finding accommodation is highly seasonal. Usually it will be little problem finding a room at short notice, but July can be well booked and it gets almost impossible to find a room anywhere near the coast as you approach 15 August. After that, pressure gradually declines, then drops considerably in September. So, of course, does the temperature.

The easiest way to find a hotel room is to visit or telephone the local tourist office (see the end of many **What to see** entries in this book for addresses and telephone numbers). If you go to the tourist office in person, they will telephone round to find you a room in the price-band of your choice.

Many Norman restaurants have rooms, and many hotels have an excellent restaurant. The hotels and restaurants mentioned in the **What to see** sections of the book are usually of this kind, especially those in small places in the country. Apart from those mentioned, there are many more, which you are likely to find by chance or inquiry. Having few big towns, Normandy has few chain hotels but hundreds of modest, typical, family-run ones such as those belonging to the **Logis de France** organisation, recognised by the yellow and green 'fireplace' sign outside. If you are touring, be sure to book your room reasonably early – ideally about 16.00hrs,

ACCOMMODATION

As well as rural cottages, Gîtes de France offer Chambres d'Hôtes – good-value bed and breakfast

and certainly by 18.00 or 19.00hrs; these family hotels do not like late arrivals. If you are staying in one place for a few days, ask about *pension* (full-board) or *demi-pension* (half-board) rates. Room rates seldom include breakfast, which may be cheaper in a café.

Apartments and Gîtes

Oddly enough, this way of taking a holiday is not well developed in Normandy, at least for foreigners. Rented summer accommodation, at the seaside at least, is geared to the French, who hire by the calendar month, 1st to 31st. With their long summer holidays, this suits them well – except when it comes to the *rentrée*, and they all try to go home at once – but for foreigners this can be too long and too constraining. Although there are now

occasional signs of shorter lets being offered, generally speaking non-French looking for a seaside house or flat to rent will have to take a travel agent's package or, perhaps, rent from a compatriot who owns a holiday house in France. Away from the sea, *gîtes ruraux* (country cottages) are popular holiday homes. Through local tourist offices or through **Gîtes de France** – a national body with offices in each *département* – you can obtain a brochure and book direct to stay in a *gîte* on a farm or in the country. These are the addresses of **Gîtes de France** in each *département*:

Seine-Maritime Chemin de la Bretèque, BP 59, 76232 Bois-Guillaume (tel: 35 60 73 34).
Eure 9 rue de la Petite Cité, BP 882, 27008 Evreux (tel: 32 39 53 38).
Orne 88 rue St-Blaise, BP 50, 61002 Alençon (tel: 33 28 88 71).
Calvados 6 promenade Mme de Sévigné, 14050 Caen (tel: 31 70 25 25).
Manche Maison du Département, 50008 St-Lô (tel: 33 05 98 70).
Gîtes de France also have an office in **England**, at 178 Piccadilly, London W1V 9DB (tel: 0171-493 3480).

Chambres d'Hôtes

'Bed and breakfast' is an established tradition in Britain, but the equivalent – Chambres d'Hôtes – is something of an innovation in France. Nevertheless, these days you will often see private houses advertising accommodation, particularly in country

areas. Whether in cottage or château, *Chambres d'Hôtes* usually offer good value and a warm welcome, and are a good way to save on hotel bills.

Many farms, cottages and châteaux now take paying guests

Camping and Caravanning
Every little French municipality feels obliged to run a campsite. There are hundreds of modest campsites throughout Normandy where you can stay without much difficulty even during the crowded summer months – the cows are just shifted on to another field when the first is full. Though they are modest, there are few campsites today that do not have a toilet block with a shower, for which you pay. High-grade, four- or five-star sites may not charge extra for showers, but their daily fee more than covers the cost of unlimited hot water. Certain organisations will arrange camping holidays where you stay only at the very best campsites. One such is **Castels et Camping-Caravaning**, BP 301, 56007 Vannes (tel: 97 42 55 83). Perhaps in the grounds of a château, such a site may have facilities such as a lake for canoeing, or organised table-tennis and other competitions. You can expect these sites to run rather strict rules like a boarding-house. In them, in an increasingly common arrangement, you can hire the tent or caravan by the week or

Mont-St-Michel – always lively

fortnight ready erected and equipped. Such sites are very popular, especially with the English and Dutch; but the only French you see are the people who run it. The **Château de Martragny**, north of Caen, is perhaps top of them all. The French camp in tents rather seldom; they use caravans and often one that remains on the site all year. As a result they tend to have their own area in every campsite anyway.

Château Stays

Château owners who have not opened a camping site sometimes convert their château into a hotel or take in paying guests. A good example is the 17th-century **Château d'Audrieu**, southeast of Bayeux, in beautiful grounds and with a famous kitchen. Others near by are **Le Castel**, and **Vaulaville**, near Tour-en-Bessin, which is more properly a stately home taking house guests. **Fervaques** in the Auge is specially for the disabled (tel: 31 32 33 96). Organisations with information available in Britain are **Château-Accueil** (94 Bell Street, Henley-on-Thames RG9 1XS tel: 0491-578803)) and **Relais Châteaux** (French Government Tourist Office, 178 Piccadilly, London W1V OAL).

Buying a House

Estate agents have prospered and multiplied in Normandy and have become quite used now to helping foreigners looking to buy. You will even find in newsagents a magazine published in English for residents and house-owners. Although the age of great bargains, if it ever existed, is over, there remain plenty of empty or abandoned houses in the Normandy countryside, which may be very pretty and cheap to buy when isolated and in poor repair, which is often the case. Selling again may be more difficult, letting is not always simple, and all sorts of bureaucratic and tax problems may arise. Take lots of advice.

CULTURE, ENTERTAINMENT AND NIGHTLIFE

The seaside resorts offer plenty of action in summer. Discos and other evening entertainment will probably be advertised in tourist offices, or will become readily apparent in these small towns once it gets late. Only Rouen has anything approaching a metropolitan culture or subculture.

At the seaside, especially, there is constant life during the season at the casinos, which usually have two classes of play – for higher stakes in the grandest room and for lower ones in other parts. The casinos are usually the venue for various special evening shows, spectacles, comedy, or other entertainments, put on by the town in the summer, especially during August. (See also **Special Events**, pages 111–12)

WEATHER AND WHEN TO GO

There is no doubt that for most people, Normandy is for summer holidays. Not only its resorts but also many of its châteaux and museums close down for the winter, and only slowly struggle into life again with the spring. The two months of the real season are July and August, and the absolute peak is the weekend around 15 August. The resorts empty very rapidly in September, and the season ends on All Saints' Day, 1 November.

One reason for this is that July and August coincide with the French school holidays. They are also the only months when you can be reasonably sure of getting good weather. Occasionally there is a summer of bad weather – though not for some years now. Usually, even if it does rain for a day or two, the temperature never falls very low and it soon clears up –

usually more rapidly on the coast than inland.

Of course, you can get good weather out of season as well. But beware of September and October – there are storms about, the rain is more frequent and harder, and you can have a whole bad week, which is much rarer in the summer. June can be a good month. Earlier in the year everywhere is less crowded, of course, but the weather may be fresh.

If you are touring and visiting places, many of them open from Easter, but with restricted days and times. In July and August you can be confident of just turning up – like everyone else, of course.

Do not write off Normandy in the winter. The food is still good, the churches are open, and you can go for a walk on the beach even if it is a bit melancholic. It can make a refreshing Christmas or New Year break, or a long weekend to liven up the bleak winter months.

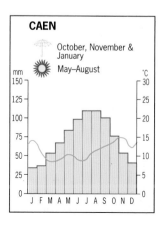

CAEN

October, November & January

May–August

Make time to stand and stare...

HOW TO BE A LOCAL

The Normans, among the French in general, are rather easy-going, content with themselves and their rich land, friendly and relaxed rather than uptight towards foreigners, and not so obsessed as the city-dwellers with elegance, dignity or money. It is not very difficult to blend in, if you are willing to drink what they drink, eat what they eat, and go along with what they think – for a while, at least.

It makes a great deal of difference, there is no denying it, whether or not you speak the language. Despite the influx of foreigners in summer, few shop assistants or bar-keepers speak another language, although if they do it will probably be English. In fact, in the last 10 years or so, the French have generally become less stuffy about speaking anyone else's language or about the way other people speak theirs, and this is still more true in easy-going Normandy. Nonetheless if you can manage the correct French to order a beer, there is a chance you may get a smile, and you should at least get a civil nod; if you can't, the reception will probably be chilly even if the waiter understands perfectly well. A little French makes things much friendlier.

For the rest, though Normandy is a different place it is not a different world. The usual north European conventions tend to apply: people respect queues, they are honest about money transactions, they expect the usual courtesies. However, they greet and expect to be greeted more than some nations, and they are accustomed to using polite appellatives such as *monsieur* and *madame* (sir and madam).

In small Norman towns one finds a lot of respect for the elderly and for the establishment figures of their slightly old-fashioned communities: many people will have lived there all their lives and are reluctant to change their ways readily. They willingly accept foreigners, however, as long as they do nothing outrageous or overbearing.

CHILDREN

Normandy is all about family holidays, and it has just about everything children could want, from A to Z – or at least from B for beaches to W for war museums.

Beaches

There is nothing like a beach to keep young children occupied for hours – and Normandy has miles of beaches, with rocks and pools full of shrimps and crabs, and above all superb sand. On many of the most popular beaches, the sea comes in shallow for paddling, and where it becomes deep is watched attentively by lifeguards. They will have a tannoy system for lost children – but if you do have to ask them for help, they will scold you terribly first.

Every municipal beach has a children's play compound or 'Mickey' (many of them take Mickey Mouse as their emblem), where there are organised games, trampolines, often swimming pools, as well as a host of activities for children up to about 10 years old. The supervisors are generally students, who are usually very good with children. The only disadvantage is that they tend to be a bit expensive. The 'Mickey' has usually closed by about 17.00hrs, and then you will often see other children enter the compound and enjoy the swings and roundabouts for free.

For older children, the larger resorts have equipment you can hire for the various seaside

Carolles-Plage in high season

sports of today such as windsurfing or beach buggying. Many seaside places also have a municipal swimming pool, sometimes covered, with which various other activities are associated, from humble ping-pong to learning how to scuba-dive. Often there is an aquarium. Sports facilities include tennis courts and mini-golf; you can usually hire a bicycle or a horse. If you have money to spend, there is lots to do, but the cost can mount up terribly – not counting the special events in the resorts. These might include castle-building competitions or formula *bille*, a race for model cars round a track built in the sand – you flick a small wooden ball (*la bille*) and move your car as far as you

Formula bille – *a game with no age barriers*

flick it, unless you flick it off the track. But these and similar activities should perhaps be in another category, headed 'Adult children'. Many of the competitors are adults (and take them very seriously), though there will be separate prizes for under-14's as well. Enquire for all these things on the spot or at the local tourist office; and look out for posters.

Inland
Inland, the four- and five-star campsites will have as many facilities as a beach, and will provide all sorts of amusements for children, including special events and competitions. Normandy is rich in forests where children can run about, picnic, cycle or ride horses. Enquire at tourist offices for the many centres for *équitation* (horse-riding). One or two châteaux have special entertainments for children, and there are a few zoos.

Museums
The numerous war museums along the D-Day coast, especially the one at Arromanches (see page 50), and the two a little inland, at Caen (page 56) and Bayeux (page 61), are wonderful for children. To them may be added, at Bayeux, the Centre Guillaume le Conquérant with the Bayeux tapestry (page 60) – organised partly with children in mind. Many smaller towns up and down Normandy have little municipal museums with displays of objects, from fishing tackle to firearms, which may capture children's imagination for an hour. A selection of these

and others – maritime museums, car museums, lace-making museums, for example – are listed in the **What to See** sections of this book, as are numerous ruined castles and abbeys, some of which have their own museums.

TIGHT BUDGET

In Normandy, like anywhere else, crowds mean higher prices. If you want to pay less, you must go where there are fewer people. The Côte Fleurie in the high season is the most expensive place in Normandy. Life is cheaper, even in July and August, on the west coast of the Cotentin (but well away from Mont-St-Michel). Prices are lower inland: you could stay somewhere outside a main resort and go in during the day. Things are also always cheaper, anywhere, out of high season.

● Shop around – not only for meals, hotels and souvenirs but also for expensive essentials like petrol. See **Shopping**, pages 101–3, for the pros and cons of *hypermarchés*, supermarkets and markets. Beware the small supermarket, probably expensive if also convenient (for instance on a campsite).

● Avoid central cafés. The cheaper one round the corner will offer a less attractive view but an equally refreshing drink.

● Study the menus that are always displayed outside restaurants, and look out for 'hidden' charges such as *couverture* (cover charge), drinks and so on, Often, some wine is included in a tourist menu. A fixed menu is often cheaper than *à la carte*.

● Watch the sundries. It is the drinks, ice-creams, tempting-looking cakes and the like – all the treats you buy when abroad and in holiday mood – that can put you over budget.

● Go diesel. French taxation remains to date extremely favourable to diesel as opposed to petrol, whether leaded or unleaded.

● Watch your speed! Speeding fines are imposed on the spot and could make a big hole in your budget, For speed limits, see page 115.

SPECIAL EVENTS

During the summer, almost every community will have something on. The tourist office will know all about it, and will have further details on the ones listed below. Travelling fairs are still a constant feature of Norman towns.

February/March *Mardi Gras* (Shrove Tuesday) Granville: carnival

April Bernay: flower festival

May Coutances: jazz festival

May Mont-St-Michel: St Michael's Fair

May (last weekend) Rouen: Joan of Arc festival

May/June (Whit Monday) Bernay: processions

June Caen: antiques fair

June Mortagne-au-Perche: music festival

June St-Pierre-sur-Dives: dressage competition

June Villedieu-les-Poêles: Grand-Sacré procession (every four years: next 1999)

July Bagnoles-de-l'Orne: 'July in Bagnoles'

Canoeing at Clécy

July Cabourg: regatta of '1000 Sails'
July Deauville: bridge (cards) festival
July Forges-les-Eaux: horse fair
July Le Havre: international regatta
July (end) Mont-St-Michel: pilgrimage processions
July (16th, at night) La-Haye-de-Routot: Le Feu de St Clair (bonfire)
July (last Sunday) Granville: blessing of sea
August Deauville: horse-racing, horse sales, polo
August Domfront: medieval festival
August (2nd Sunday) Le Havre: flower festival
August (mid) Barneville-Carteret: 'Fêtes de la Mer'
August (mid) Dieppe: carnival
August (mid) Lisieux: religious procession
August (late) Cabourg/Dives-sur-Mer: William the Conqueror festival
September (early) Deauville: festival of American films
September (early) Lessay: St Cross fair

September Alençon: music festival
September Caen: horse-racing and fair
September Caudebec: cider festival (alternate years)
September Louviers: St Michael's fair
September (end) Mont-St-Michel: St Michael's fair
September (last weekend) Lisieux: festival of Ste Thérèse
October (early) Deauville: vintage car rally, Paris-Deauville
October (mid) Vimoutiers: apple festival
October/November Rouen: St Romain's fair
November Dieppe: herring festival
December St Valéry-en-Caux: herring and cider festival

SPORT

All sorts of beach and countryside sports are available in Normandy: in particular there are numerous golf-courses and horse-riding stables (enquire at the local tourist office or at your hotel). Temporary use or membership of golf-courses, tennis courts, swimming pools and the like usually possible: the fee will be more than minimal but not outrageous. Equipment such as bicycles, canoes and wind-surfing boards can be hired, though again not cheaply. Apart from these the most common local sport is the very farmerly one of *balltrap* (clay-pigeon shooting). Special competitions, from table-tennis to sandcastle making, are put on in resorts in summer (see **Children**, pages 109–11).

Directory

This section (with the biscuit-coloured band) contains day-to-day information, including travel, health and documentation.

Contents

Arriving

Although there are small airports at Caen, Cherbourg, Deauville, Rouen and Le Havre, most people enter Normandy by land or sea or, now, tunnel.

Ferries

Ferries from England (Poole, Southampton, Portsmouth and Newhaven) and Ireland (Cork and Rosslare) dock at Caen, Cherbourg, Le Havre and Dieppe. All these crossings take at least four hours, and many British cross to Calais or Boulogne and drive to Normandy. This is an even better option using the Channel Tunnel, since the link roads in northern France have been greatly improved. During August it is wise, if not essential, to book ferries in advance.

Road and Rail

The motorway (A13) between Paris and Caen (with extensions to Le Havre and Deauville), continues with mostly dual carriageway (N13) up to Cherbourg.

Fast trains run from Paris (St-Lazare and Montparnasse stations) to Rouen and some other towns. Travelling within Normandy by train often involves changing.

Entry Formalities

For a stay of up to three months, nationals of Britain, Ireland and other EU countries, the USA, Canada and New Zealand need only a passport. Check, though, with a travel agent or the French Government Tourist Office (for addresses see **Tourist Offices**, page 125), since visa policy is subject to review.

Camping

Normandy is excellent for camping. It is full of campsites of all sorts and sizes, from the basic *camping à la ferme* (farm) or municipal sites to four-star sites, usually taking both tents and caravans, and often hiring tents or caravans ready in place (see **Accommodation**, page 105). Details of sites can be obtained at local tourist offices or, before you travel, in specialist books or agency brochures. In summer, arrive early at the site to be sure of a place. If you do, it is seldom necessary to book.

Cars see Driving

Chemist see Pharmacies

Crime

This need not be uppermost in your mind in Normandy, but take elementary precautions such as locking the car and not leaving valuables visible.

Customs Regulations

The standard EU regulations apply. See also **Entry Formalities** above.

Disabled Travellers

In most public places these days in Normandy there are ramps as well as steps, and a fair amount has been done to make buildings accessible to wheelchair visitors.

Driving

A certain amount of preparation is required for British and Irish drivers – not least gearing yourself up for driving on the right.

Insurance

Special insurance should be taken out – a current comprehensive car insurance policy will cover you for third-party risks abroad, but for comprehensive insurance you will need a 'green card', which you can arrange direct or through your broker at home. You may also wish to take out special accident, illness, loss or breakdown cover (such as AA Five Star Europe), which can be invaluable – especially if you don't speak French or are unfamiliar with the country.

Documents

You should carry with you a valid full driving licence (international permit not required for visitors from the US, UK or Western Europe); a current insurance certificate; the vehicle's registration document, and a letter from the vehicle's owner giving you permission to drive it if the owner is not accompanying the vehicle.

Headlights

Beam deflectors or headlamp converters (available from the AA or car accessory shops) should be fixed to your headlights, for otherwise they will be dipping into oncoming traffic rather than away from it.

A view worth a detour any day – Les Andelys on the Seine

The French like their headlights yellow, and it is possible to stick on a yellow filter or paint the glass with a special yellow lacquer, but this is not so important.

Other Accessories
Your car should display a nationality plate or sticker, usually provided with your ferry ticket. Extras to carry with you include a complete spare-bulb kit for your vehicle and an emergency warning triangle.

Seat-belts
Laws are the same as in Britain.

Speed Limits
Speed limits on French roads are sometimes lower than on the equivalent roads in other countries. They are zealously enforced by the police using radar traps and heavy on-the-spot fines to deter offenders. The speed limit in towns and villages is 50kph (31mph), or sometimes lower – watch for signs. Ordinary roads – even dead straight ones with no traffic – have a limit of 90kph (55mph). On dual carriageways and non-toll motorways you can travel at 110kph (68mph), while on toll motorways the speed limit rises to 130kph (80mph). In rain or other bad weather the speed limits automatically reduce from 90 to 80kph, from 110 to 100kph and from 130 to 110kph. There is also a *minimum* speed limit of 80kph (49mph) for the outside lane of a level stretch of motorway in good daytime visibility.

Drinking and Driving
By far the safest policy is not to drive after drinking alcohol. Apart from increasing the risk of an accident spoiling your holiday, you risk an instant and heavy fine if you are found to be over the limit. French law entitles the police to take random breath tests.

Road Signs

France uses the normal international road signs. *Chaussée déformée* means an uneven road surface. *Chantier* or *Travaux* means roadworks.

Giving Way

This is perhaps the hardest part about driving in France, and it is well worth becoming thoroughly familiar with the necessary road signs.

In towns the rule of *priorité à droite* prevails. Unless a notice says otherwise, you must give way to any vehicle crossing from your right, even from small side-roads. As a corollary, you will often have the right of way when you did not expect it, and you will only annoy French drivers by stopping.

The priority rule at roundabouts no longer applies, which means you give way to traffic already on the roundabout. You are reminded by the signs *Vous n'avez pas la priorité* (You do not have priority), or *Cédez le passage* (Give way). Outside the towns, important main roads have right of way. This is indicated by one of three road signs:

1 A red-bordered triangle surrounding a black cross on a white background with the words *Passage protégé* (You have right of way).

2 A red-bordered triangle with a pointed black upright with a horizontal bar on a white background.

3 A yellow diamond within a white diamond. (The yellow diamond crossed through means 'you no longer have priority'.)

Pay attention to road markings, and do not cross a solid white or yellow line marked on the centre of the road.

Traffic lights also need special care. They can be dim, and are sometimes high above the road. A flashing amber light warns of a particularly dangerous junction.

Accidents

Follow the instructions given by your insurance company. Ask any witnesses to stay in order to make statements, and contact the police. Exchange insurance details with other drivers involved.

Breakdowns

Carry a red warning triangle, and if you break down place it on the road 33 yards (30m) behind the broken-down vehicle. Switch on your hazard warning lights.

France has no nationwide road assistance service such as the AA, so seek help from a local garage in the event of a breakdown. (It is wise to take out emergency breakdown insurance before you leave home. Read the accompanying instructions carefully, and keep them handy in the car in case you break down.) Emergency phones (marked 'SOS'), where they exist, are connected direct to the police, who will contact a garage for you.

Car Rental

This is perfectly possible, though not particularly cheap in France. It may be less expensive to arrange and pay for it before you travel to France.

Fuel

Most petrol stations now take credit cards as well as cash. All except the most old-fashioned pumps in remote villages offer unleaded petrol (*essence sans plomb*). Check the octane rating your car requires.

For a full tank, ask for *le plein, s'il vous plaît*. Expect to pay more than average for petrol on an *autoroute*, less than average at a *hypermarché*.

Some petrol stations now have an unmanned night service with a pump that works like a cash-dispensing machine in requiring a PIN number as well as the credit card. This is a pity for foreigners, for it may not recognise their PIN. Nor will it take cash. If desperate, you could wait for a Frenchman to come along and then offer him cash in exchange for his using his credit card on your behalf.

Electricity

The supply is 220 volts. Plugs have two or sometimes three round pins. Adaptors for French plugs are not easy to find in France, and are best bought before leaving home.

Embassies and Consulates

British Embassy

35 rue du Faubourg-St-Honoré, 75383 Paris (tel: 1-42 66 91 42), with a consular section at 9 avenue Hoche, 75008 Paris (tel: 1-42 66 38 10). There are British Consulates with Honorary Consuls in Cherbourg and Le Havre.

US Embassy

2 avenue Gabriel, 75382 Paris (tel: 1-42 96 12 02)

Canadian Embassy

35 avenue Montaigne, 75008 Paris (tel: 1-47 23 01 01)

Irish Embassy

4 rue Rude, 75016 Paris (tel: 1-45 00 20 87)

Australian Embassy

4 rue Jean Rey, 75015 Paris (tel: 1-40 59 33 07)

New Zealand Embassy

Rue Léonard-da-Vinci, Paris (tel: 1-45 00 24 11)

Emergency Telephone Numbers

Police 17
Firemen (*Sapeurs pompiers*) 18
Ambulance Number given in telephone call-box; otherwise telephone the Police (17).

Entertainment Information

The local tourist office is the best source of information. See also **Culture, Entertainment and Nightlife**, pages 106–7.

Health

No special precautions or vaccinations are required. In the event of illness (rather than an emergency requiring an ambulance – see **Emergency Telephone Numbers**, above), doctors

Carriage display at Haras du Pin

(*médecins*) and dentists (*dentistes*) can be found by enquiry at the tourist office (which can also give you a list beforehand) or in the telephone directory.

You will have to pay for treatment, but, under a reciprocal health agreement between Britain and France, the British can reclaim most of the doctor's fee and also prescription charges.

To do this, you need to take with you to France a form E111, obtainable from post offices on completion of the form contained in booklet 'T2'. Obtain a form (*feuille de soins*) from the French doctor and send it and the receipts of payment to the local *Caisse Primaires d'Assurance-Maladie*. Check with the doctor or the tourist office which *Caisse* to send them to. The Irish can obtain a similar dispensation by applying to their Regional Health Board at home for a form E111.

Normandy is not free from that bane of the summer holiday, the mosquito, but insect repellents of all kinds are available from pharmacies or *quincailleries* (ironmongers). Wasps may also be a problem for picnickers.

If you are on the beach, be very careful about sunburn and sunstroke. Take special care with young children, ensuring they wear sunhats and a sun-screening cream. Acclimatise yourselves to the sun gradually, and do not underestimate the burning power of hazy sunshine, especially if there is a sea breeze.

Holidays

French public and religious holidays are:
New Year's Day (1 January)
Easter Sunday and Monday
Labour Day (1 May)
VE Day (8 May)
Ascension Day (40 days after Easter)
Whitsun or Pentecost – Sunday and Monday
Bastille Day (14 July)
Assumption (15 August)
All Saints' Day (1 November)
Remembrance Day (11 November)
Christmas Day (25 December)

Lost Property

In Normandy, it will be worth returning to the place where you lost anything – a restaurant, shop, hotel, place on the beach – and enquiring, because people are usually honest and glad to help. The police are perhaps less interested in finding lost property than they might be – but inform them if documents such as a passport, credit cards or cheques are involved. For passports, also inform your embassy (see **Embassies and Consulates**, page 117). Make sure you have kept a note of what to do if you lose your credit cards or travellers' cheques (see **Credit Cards**, page 120).

Media

All kinds of brochures and leaflets are available at the tourist office, and local papers will advertise everything going on. In well-frequented towns in summer you can be sure to find a newsagent carrying a good stock of foreign as well as French newspapers (the local

one is *Ouest-France*), also a range of local maps and guides, informing about everything from walks to restaurants.

Radio and Television
You should be able to receive most BBC radio stations in Normandy. *Radio France Normandie* can be heard on 102.6 MHz and there are a number of local stations. French hotels are rather behind other European countries in providing a range of national channels for the television in your room.

Money
The French franc (FF) is the unit of currency. There are silver coins for 50 centimes (½ franc), 1 franc, 2 francs and 5 francs. The 10 and 20-franc coins are brass with a silver centre, and there are brass coins for 20, 10 and 5 centimes. Banknotes start at 20 francs, then 50, 100 and 200 francs.

Something for everyone – this bakery sells many different breads

There is no limit to the currency that may be imported or, in practice, exported.

Exchange
On balance, to get the best rate most conveniently, it is advisable to change money into French francs before you travel to France. If you don't want to take all your money in cash, or need a standby in case of emergency or overspending, Eurocheques (obtainable from your bank at home) are the next best thing. However, it is often cheapest (in terms of exchange rates and commission) and most convenient to pay at hotels, shops, petrol-stations and restaurants with a credit card where possible – which is most places. Eurocheques, travellers' cheques and cash can be changed at most banks, which

DIRECTORY

often have a special desk for exchange. Fortunately the old system where you did the paper transaction at one desk and then went to the *caisse* to get the cash, is becoming extinct. Bank opening hours are 09.00 (or sometimes earlier) to 12.00hrs, then 14.00 (or 14.45) to 16.00 (or 16.45) hrs. Banks are closed on Sunday and either Saturday or Monday. However, in small towns inland you may well find that some banks are only part-time, opening on alternate days, for instance, or only in the mornings. The only way to be sure is to check on the spot.

If a bank is impracticable, then ports, airports, ferries and main railway stations have exchange facilities, but rates are poor. It is usually said that hotels also give poor rates, but if you are staying or eating there they are often happy, these days, to give you the bank rate or even better. Nowadays the whole business is much less fraught than it used to be.

In Deauville the beach-tents face the boardwalk rather than out to sea

Bank and Credit Cards

Even shops that don't advertise the fact often take credit cards these days. However, some *hypermarchés* don't. Many cash dispensers will now recognise foreign PIN numbers with credit cards, and this can be a handy method of obtaining cash quickly. The French usually authenticate every kind of purchase by tapping in their PIN, and some outlets may demand you do so, but explain (and insist) that your card works differently. The French *Carte Bleue* is the equivalent of Visa; Access or Mastercard is also called Eurocard. Nowadays credit card insurance is well worth having, above all because it reduces the complications of informing the necessary offices of loss or theft.

Eurocheques

Virtually every hotel or shop, including *hypermarchés*, will accept a Eurocheque with its accompanying card. You can also draw money at a bank up to the value of FF1400 per cheque. Be warned that if you make out a cheque for more than this amount, even though it

is legitimate (though not guaranteed), you become liable for a much steeper commission with your bank at home. The payee also often has to pay charges, which is the reason why Eurocheques may occasionally be refused.

Opening Times

Banks see **Money**, above.

Bars Times vary, but there are no compulsory closure times. Most are open all day except on one day (*jour de repos*) a week.

Museums, châteaux, etc Tuesday is the usual day on which state museums shut, and many municipal and private institutions follow suit. But not necessarily: Monday is another common closing day, followed by Wednesday or Friday. Most institutions close altogether in mid-winter. Many open every day during July and August. Some close on public holidays, others open specially for them. Indications are given in the individual entries in the **What to See** sections of this book. Many places close for lunch – usually from 12.00 to 14.00hrs. Few stay open after 17.00hrs, though some close at 18.00hrs in high season.

Post Offices see **Post Office**, page 122

Restaurants Most close at least one day a week, sometimes one and a half days. Many of the smartest take their holidays during high season, not off season. They vary enormously, so enquire by telephone.

Shops The usual times are from about 09.00hrs (dry goods shops are often later, *boulangeries* earlier) to 12.00hrs, or 12.30hrs in the case of food shops. Lunchtime closing is normal. Shops re-open between 14.00 and 15.00hrs, and stay open (and this is really useful) till 19.00, 19.30 or even 20.00hrs (often depending on business). In Normandy, there are seasonal exceptions: in high season shops will usually open longer and more often (*boulangeries* often forego their weekly closing day), and in low season they will close more readily. Quite a lot of shops, especially *boulangeries* and *pâtisseries*, open on Sunday morning, closing on Monday morning instead. Many shops do not open, or open late after stock-taking, on Monday morning. *Hypermarchés* often stay open during the lunch-hour (they have cafés and restaurants), and until 21.00 or 22.00hrs. They are closed on Sunday and sometimes also on Monday morning.

Tourist Offices The usual hours are 9.00 to 19.00hrs, either closing for lunch or operating with minimal staff. Tourist offices very often close down as such during the winter; or rather, in many places, they are set up for the summer. In smaller places, even in the season, their opening hours are erratic and they may open only on certain days, though they are usually open in the morning.

Personal Safety

Normandy being mostly rural, or at least free from most of the evils of the big city, personal safety is not something requiring special care.

DIRECTORY

Pharmacies

French pharmacies, identifiable by the green cross suspended outside, emanate a wonderful air of cleanliness and efficiency, and usually manage to be friendly as well as clinical. They frequently offer a bewildering range of beauty products in their window, besides the drugs and medicines which the pharmacist is empowered to prescribe, if necessary, for minor ailments. Often they will speak some English.

In case of emergency, the prescribing doctor will tell you which pharmacies will be open outside normal hours. The rota of *pharmacies de garde*, as they are called, is listed in tourist office handouts, in local newspapers, at the police station, or on the door even of closed pharmacies.

Places of Worship

For anything other than a Catholic mass in French, enquire at the tourist office. Masses are listed on church doors, and sometimes still on signs as you enter towns or villages.

Police

There is a distinction between the *police municipale*, or local police, who also fulfil the functions of various kinds of 'wardens', and the *gendarmes*, who deal with crime and also traffic offences (usually on the open road rather than in a town). *Gendarmes* carry guns. You are most likely to get involved with either sort as a result of traffic offences. You will find them strict, inclined neither to discuss the case nor to let

you go; on the other hand they won't moralise tediously, they will just fine you (often on the spot). See also **Driving**, pages 114–17.

An important figure on the beaches is not a policeman (indeed, he is often little more than a student), but the lifeguard. He is responsible for order and safety on the beach and in the sea, and his word is law.

Post Office

Central or branch post offices, or PTT (*Poste et Télécommunications*), are usually open from 08.00 to 19.00hrs on weekdays and from 08.00 to 12.00hrs on Saturdays (branch offices may well close at lunchtime). They will send a telex or fax, also telegrams. They should also – like most hotels and many private subscribers – have a 'minitel', or computerised telephone book: it is better than a telephone book in doing many more kinds of searches.

All towns and districts are now post-coded. When addressing a letter, write the code before the name of the town.

Poste restante only operates in main post offices in major towns. Address the letter: Poste Restante, Poste Centrale, followed by the town name. Stamps are sold in post offices but can also be bought in a *tabac* (tobacconist's). Letter boxes are yellow.

Public Transport

Getting about between towns and villages in Normandy is not very easy. The railways tend to radiate from Paris, so getting across Normandy can involve one or often more changes, with long intervals. The local bus service may well be more direct; enquire locally. Within large towns, such as Rouen or Caen, buses again can be used; in most cases you need to buy the ticket beforehand. Taxis are not very expensive, if you can find them at the taxi rank (you can usually obtain a taxi call number at a hotel, restaurant or shop). For air and ferries, see **Arriving**, page 113.

Senior Citizens
Normandy is full of locals who have lived there all their lives, or families who have been holidaying in Normandy for generations. People also like to retire to some of the resorts. Given the traditionalism of manners and mores, Normandy is an excellent place for senior citizens, who will be welcomed and respected. Reductions are available for nationals of EU countries on rail travel and on other communal charges: enquire at the Department of Social Security, at railway station enquiry offices at home, and at tourist offices both at home and in Normandy.

Student and Youth Travel
For reductions on travel into and around Normandy, enquire at student or youth travel organisations at home for qualifications. The French National Youth Hostel Association (*Fédération Unie des Auberges de Jeunesse – FUJA*) is at 27 rue Pajol, 75018 Paris (tel: 1-46 07 00 01). Normandy is full of campsites

(see **Camping**). It is quite possible to go on a walking, cycling or driving tour of Normandy and camp and eat very cheaply if you are hardy.

Telephones
The dialling tone is a long, sharp hum. The ringing tone is a long slow burr, followed by a pause and more long slow burrs. The engaged tone (*occupé*) consists of more rapid burrs. To telephone into Normandy from abroad, dial the international code (00 from Britain), then 33, then the eight figures of the number required. To telephone within Normandy or to the rest of France, dial just the eight figures. To dial Paris, prefix the eight figures with 161. To dial Normandy from Paris, dial 16 then the eight-figure number. To dial out of France from Normandy, dial 19 and wait for a new tone. Then dial the international code of the country you want (for example

Capturing the view, Mont-St-Michel

DIRECTORY

Formal gardens at Thury Harcourt

1 for the United States and Canada; 44 for Britain; 353 for Ireland; 61 for Australia; 64 for New Zealand), then the local code (omitting the initial zero) and number. A series of rapid pips means you are being connected.

For directory enquiries, dial 12. Cheap rate (50 per cent cheaper) is on weekdays between 21.30 and 08.00hrs, and weekends after 14.00hrs on Saturday.

Public Telephones

Public call boxes are quite frequent. More and more only take a phone card (*télécarte*), which can be obtained in post offices, *tabacs*, newsagents and other outlets that advertise the fact. Put the card in and close the flap before dialling.

Time

France follows Greenwich Mean Time plus one hour, except during summer time (late March to late September) which is plus two hours. French time is the same time as the rest of Europe except Britain and Ireland, which are one hour behind all year (except for a short interval in October, when they are the same).

Tipping

Service is nearly always *compris* (included) these days in hotel, bar and restaurant bills. However, it remains a friendly gesture to leave small change in the waiter's saucer in bars and restaurants. Some people still tip taxi drivers, but it is not expected. Hotel maids may deserve to be tipped with money left in the room.

Toilets

The usual international symbols are used for Ladies, Gents and Disabled toilets. You will still sometimes see *Dames* (Women) and *Messieurs* (Gentlemen) or *Hommes* (Men). You will still find 'squat' toilets, said to be much better for you, in many places, but they make up a diminishing percentage, well under half. You will also find, in places like Deauville, high-tech toilets that do not just flush the bowl but clean the seat as well. Children love them as much as they hate the 'squat' toilets, if they are not used to them, but you have to pay at least two francs.

Public toilets exist (often, very usefully for children, on beaches) but for these, too, you will have to pay the *concierge*. Otherwise you may ask to use the toilet in a bar, a request that will surely be granted, but do leave a tip or buy a drink.

Tourist Offices

The telephone numbers and addresses of the invaluable local *Offices de Tourisme* or *Syndicats d'Initiative* are given under town entries in the **What to See** sections of this book. These tourist offices provide plenty of information, leaflets or brochures, ranging from entertainment to street maps. There are also regional and *département* tourist offices, but they tend to provide only much broader information:

For All Normandy Comité Régional de Tourisme de Normandie, 14 rue Charles-Corbeau, 27000 Evreux (tel: 32 33 79 00)

Seine-Maritime Comité Départemental de Tourisme (CDT), 2 bis rue du Petit-Salut, BP 680, 76008 Rouen (tel: 35 88 61 32)

Eure CDT, Hôtel du Département, boulevard Georges-Chauvin, 27021 Evreux (tel: 32 31 51 51)

Orne CDT, 88 rue St-Blaise, BP 50, 61002 Alençon (tel: 33 28 88 71)

Calvados CDT, place du Canada, 14000 Caen (tel: 31 86 53 30)

Manche CDT, Maison du Département, route de Villedieu, 50008 St-Lô (tel: 33 05 98 70). These are perhaps best for information about accommodation or letting. But French Government Tourist Offices abroad will supply this and are probably more attuned to providing individual orientation and travel details for that particular country:

Britain 178 Piccadilly, London W1V OAL, (tel: 0171-491 7622; 24-hour recorded information 0171-499 6911) 0891 - 244123.

Ireland 35 Lower Abbey Street, Dublin 1 (tel: 01-771 871)

USA 610 Fifth Avenue, New York, NY 10020 (tel: 212/757 1125); or 645 Michigan Avenue, Chicago, Ill 60611 (tel: 312/337 6301); or 9454 Wilshire Boulevard, Suite 314, Beverley Hills, Ca 90212 (tel: 310/271 6665); or 2305 Cedar Springs Boulevard, Dallas, Texas 75201 (tel: 214/720 4010)

Canada 1981 Avenue McGill College, Suite 490, Montréal, Québec H3A 2W9 (tel: 514/288 4264)

Australia BNP Building, 12th Floor, 12 Castelreagh Street, Sydney NSW 2000 (tel: 02-231 5244).

The sort of information tourist offices usually provide includes how to get there; lists and prices of hotels, campsites, restaurants; services; events; information on what to visit .

Travel Agencies in Normandy

These are almost all geared for French use, and international travel; some will provide Intercity railway tickets.

LANGUAGE

French people always appreciate it if you try to speak to them in their own language. Courtesy is all-important: prefix questions to strangers with *s'il vous plaît* or *excusez-moi*, and address people as *monsieur* or *madame*.

please s'il vous plaît
thank you merci
hello bonjour
good evening/night bonsoir
goodbye au revoir
I'm sorry pardon
yes/no oui/non
today aujourd'hui
yesterday hier
open ouvert
closed fermé
big grand
small petit
hot chaud
cold froid
excuse me excusez-moi
can you direct me to...? pouvez-vous m'indiquer la direction de...?
where is...? où se trouve...?
toilets les toilettes
how much is it? c'est combien?
I want to buy je voudrais acheter
that's too expensive c'est trop cher
do you speak English? parlez-vous anglais?
I don't understand je ne comprends pas
could you speak more slowly? pouvez-vous parler plus lentement, s'il vous plaît?
the bill, please l'addition, s'il vous plaît
I need a doctor je voudrais voir un docteur
call an ambulance appelez une ambulance s'il vous plaît

Numbers

one un/une
two deux
three trois
four quatre
five cinq
six six
seven sept
eight huit
nine neuf
ten dix
fifty cinquante
one hundred cent
one thousand mille

Days of the Week

Monday lundi
Tuesday mardi
Wednesday mercredi
Thursday jeudi
Friday vendredi
Saturday samedi
Sunday dimanche

Shopping

shops les magasins
baker la boulangerie
newsagents, paper shop, stationers la librairie
library la bibliothèque
butcher la boucherie
chemist la pharmacie
delicatessen la charcuterie
food shop l'alimentation
fishmongers la poissonnerie
grocer's l'épicerie
cake shop la pâtisserie
post office le bureau de poste
supermarket le supermarché

Garage

brakes les freins
engine le moteur
starter le démarreur
ignition l'allumage
steering la direction
clutch l'embrayage
headlights les phares
flat tyre un pneu crevé

INDEX

Acknowledgements

The Automobile Association wishes to thank the following photographers and libraries for their assistance in the preparation of this book.

CLIVE SAWYER and R MOORE took all the photographs (© AA Photo Library), except:

P HOLBERTON 110 Formula *bille*.

MARY EVANS PICTURE LIBRARY 7 bathing, 14 Jeanne d'Arc, 18 Gustave Flaubert.

NATURE PHOTOGRAPHERS LTD 91 sea spurge, 94 perennial centaury, 96 bush cricket (all P R Sterry), 92 warbler (M Bolton), 95 lady's tresses (A J Cleave).

SPECTRUM COLOUR LIBRARY Cover: Mont-St-Michel, 30 St Valéry-en-Caux, 32 Varengeville-sur-Mer, 36 St-Maclou Cloisters, 38 Rouen.